Best in Class

Also by Adrian Plass

Best in Plass

STORIES, SONGS, POEMS & SKETCHES
by Adrian Plass

Internationally
BESTSELLING AUTHOR
ADRIAN PLASS

ZONDERVAN®

ZONDERVAN.com/
AUTHORTRACKER
follow your favorite authors

ZONDERVAN

Best in Plass
Copyright © 2010 by Adrian Plass

Cabbages for the King
Copyright © 1993 by Adrian Plass
Illustrations Copyright © 1993 by Ben Ecclestone

Clearing Away the Rubbish
Copyright © 1988 by Adrian Plass

Requests for information should be addressed to:

Zondervan, Grand Rapids, Michigan 49530

ISBN 978-0-310-29342-2

Cover design: Kristi Smith / Juicebox Designs
Interior design: Michelle Espinoza

Printed in the United States of America

10 11 12 13 14 15 16 • 23 22 21 20 19 18 17 16 15 14 13 12 11 10 9 8 7 6 5 4 3 2 1

Contents

You, Me and Us

I Know What You're Going to Say

Redundant Rituals and Flimsy Fashions

Book 2: Clearing Away the Rubbish

Cut-Price Christianity!

Hope Is Hopeless!

Book 1:

Cabbages for the King

To the Reader

Why is this first part of *Best in Plass* called *Cabbages for the King*?

The simple answer is that, on one very important level, being a Christian who happens to speak and write about his faith is much the same as being a Christian who happens to run a greengrocer's shop.

The conscientious greengrocer buys and sells the best produce he can get, in as pleasant a manner as possible, at a price that is appropriate to the resources of his customers and the needs of his own family. He does not (unless he is a greengrocer with private means) have the option of not coming in to work on those mornings when he feels spiritually barren. The public need their cabbages, and an unsanctified cabbage tastes much the same as a sanctified one. The believing greengrocer is an ordinary man trying to live up to his high calling. Day by day he does his best to provide people with what they need, and asks God to protect his customers and himself from his own shortcomings.

So do I.

When the greengrocer and I arrive in heaven together, we shall be equal in the eyes of God, except that I (hopefully) will be known by my fruit, whereas he will be known by his fruit *and* veg.

This book is a collection of the jokes, stories, sketches and verse that I, and more recently my wife and I, have flung at people from platforms all over the country. Most of them are humorous (or are supposed to be), a few are sad or serious, and the rest are beyond definition.

Such as they are, they are what I do for God – cabbages for the King. I hope you enjoy them.

Telling the Truth

Truth enters the mind so easily that when we hear it for the first time it seems as if we were simply recalling it to memory.

Bernard de Fontenelle (1768)

Truths and roses have thorns about them.

H. G. Bohn (*Handbook of Proverbs*, 1855)

Truth stretches but does not break.

Spanish proverb

Telling the Truth

How do you start a book? I never know how to start anything. Quite often, when I stand up to speak in churches or halls or theatres, I haven't the faintest idea what I'm going to say. This doesn't matter so much nowadays because I don't get as frightened as I used to, but in the early days my nervous system took a terrible pounding every time.

Recently, after arriving at a venue by the skin of my teeth, I began with the following words:

'I just want to thank my lucky stars that …'

I stopped as I realized that among those present there would almost certainly be a number who were astrologically challenged. Most people laughed when I changed my remark to: 'I just want to thank the Lord that …', but some did not.

Oh, dear!

Apart from the fact that I'm constitutionally incapable of putting together a logical sequence of ideas or points and then sticking to it (my tangential tendencies do occasionally cause a little conflict when my wife and I are working together), this inability to find a starting place is probably something to do with identity. I don't seem to fit into any of the traditional categories of Christian speaker. I'm not a preacher, I'm certainly not a Bible teacher and it's a long time since I've been allowed to just entertain. What I do have is a determination to live, privately and publicly, with the gap between what I am and what I think I ought to be. I don't mean that I won't change for the better – God is always making that possible in our lives – but I refuse to pretend that my virtue or spirituality is cubed just because I'm standing on a platform.

We shall never match our message, so I think it is probably more useful to tell the truth. Enthusiasm and optimism are no substitutes for reality.

I remember working with an evangelist in the Midlands once. It was an evening meeting and the large hall in which we were operating was about half full. I went on stage first and spoke for fifteen minutes or so, then he came on to do the main talk. Now, for those who don't know, evangelists are a fine body of men, but they find it very difficult to believe that anyone can absorb, or understand any piece of information unless it has been repeated about thirty-nine times. This fellow was no exception. When, in retrospect, I add this tendency to the aforementioned inability to separate personal and divine truth, what followed was not really very surprising. I can't remember the exact wording of my colleague's address, but here is an approximation of one whole chunk of what he said.

'I don't worry, because I belong to God. I belong to God, so I don't have to worry. Why don't I worry? Well, it's because I belong to God. Who do I belong to? It's God, of course, and because of that I don't have to worry. Worry? Me? I don't! Why should I when I belong to God? You see, belonging to God means the end of worry, and that's something I don't do now that I belong to God ...'

Several permutations later the evangelist concluded his talk, left the stage, and came into the wings where I was waiting. His whispered words took my breath away.

'I'm really worried,' he said hoarsely, 'I don't think I got through to them at all.'

I was shocked. I hadn't been in the crinkly-eyed business

for very long and I still believed that – by and large – Christian speakers were honest about themselves.

'Hold on a minute,' I replied, 'you just told all those people out there that you don't worry because you belong to God. What about that?'

'Ah, well,' he said, 'I was preaching then.'

It's so easy to get carried away like that. I've done it myself. But, balanced against experiences like the one I've just mentioned, which might make one very cynical, are some overwhelming truths.

First, nothing has changed. The message always was going to be greater than we are. John the Baptist, languishing in Herod's prison, wanted to know if Jesus really was 'the one'. Only a short time ago, filled with the Holy Spirit, he had confidently identified the Messiah in front of crowds of people at the river bank. Now, crouched in the confining darkness, faced with his own limitations, he felt wretchedly uncertain.

God uses inadequate people. He has to. They're the only sort available to choose from. He is committed to the risk of entrusting his earthly image to idiots like you, me, and my evangelist friend, people who will fail and make mistakes from time to time.

Secondly, there are many wonderful and authentically God-inspired events and miracles happening in the Church nowadays. Sadly human nature is such that many people notice absurdity, failure and vain empire-building much more readily than the things of God. You, me and the evangelist had better work even harder to keep silliness to a minimum.

There's an illustration often used in philosophical discussions on the subject of creativity. It concerns a cynic who rips apart a beautiful picture.

'I told you so!' he exclaims triumphantly. 'There is no

19

picture here. It's just a collection of wood, canvas, nails and pigment. You're all deceiving yourselves!'

He's wrong, of course. There *is* a picture, and it's so much more than the sum of its component parts.

The Church, the body of Christ, is exactly the same. Any cynic could examine my life, or the strange antics of my Christian brothers and sisters, and say, 'There's nothing here – there's just Adrian Plass and these other ridiculous bits and pieces. There *is* no Church. There is no body of Christ. There is no God!'

How sadly wrong he would be. The bride, the body, the face and hands of God on earth, quickened by the Holy Spirit, and led by the mind and will of Jesus himself must be a beautiful picture when it's viewed from heaven. God loves to look at this work of art, and I'm so glad he's painted me into one small corner.

He has given me permission to be honest about him *and* myself, and that's what I shall go on doing.

It seems very fitting that this first selection of pieces should be concerned with Truth, because Truth is the wholesaler from whom most of my 'cabbages' are obtained.

Am I the Only One?

One of my greatest fears as a young Christian was that, by some impossible means, the person I really was inside would be revealed to all the other people in my church. What would they say and think when they saw the swamp that my mind often became? How would they cope with the knowledge that I stopped believing in God altogether sometimes, or that my daily 'quiet time' was not daily at all, but weekly, or fortnightly, or monthly, or even less frequent than that? Could they accommodate a mess?

Nowadays I'm much less bothered about people knowing what I'm really like, but I shall always experience a slight sense of loneliness about being the only person, in terms of personality and outlook, who is my unique shape. I will never find another me to compare notes with (what a blessed relief for the rest of the world!), but, unique as each of us is, we do all have an awful lot in common. In fact, it can be breathtakingly liberating to discover that you are *not* 'the only one'.

AM I THE ONLY ONE?

Am I the only one
Who follows God,
Nottingham Forest,
Neighbours

And his own inclinations – usually in reverse order?
I do hope not.

Am I the only one
Who likes Norman Wisdom films,
Bat Out of Hell,
Little House on the Prairie,
and *Silence of the Lambs?*
Probably.

Am I the only one
Who hasn't learned to drive,
Probably never will,
Doesn't want to,
And might well murder the next person who asks why
    not?
Maybe.

Am I the only one
Who checks his sitting-room carpet for big bits before
    hoovering it
Then afterwards finds the suction pipe blocked with
    dead dogs,
Half bricks, rolls of prairie wire, nests of tiddly winks,
Most of the *Sunday Times* and six pound fifty in small
    change?
I doubt it.

Am I the only one
Who talks to himself loudly when he's alone
Then suddenly realizes he isn't,
Feels like a loony,
And tries to make it sound like a song?
Surely not.

Am I the only one
Who hates all criticism,
Especially the constructive sort,
Because that usually means
I have to do something about it?
I don't think so.

Am I the only one
Who likes to have his cake,
Eat it,
Sick it up,
Then feel sorry for himself?
Possibly.

Am I the only one
Who loves and needs love,
And fails and falls and cries,
And takes the hand of anyone whose turn it is to be
    strong,
Whose turn it is to be Jesus for me?
Am I the only one?

Jenny

I wish that, as a Church, we were more willing to share our shadows as well as our shining. What a shadowy event the crucifixion must have been – and what a shining outcome.

People can accept the *whole* story, however grainy and granular it may seem, much more readily than a carefully edited one.

Not long after Jenny Larcombe was miraculously healed (only those who did not know her before and after her healing could doubt that) the sister of a very close friend of ours committed suicide after years of depressive illness. She happened to be called Jenny too. She was a follower of Jesus, struggling against all the odds to remain stable enough to lead a normal life. She tried very hard, but in the end she failed, just as those who are suffering from severe physical illnesses quite often fail to recover. I would like the Church to own *both* of these Jennys, because they both belong to Jesus, equal citizens in the kingdom of God.

Of course the mystery remains, but it is a mystery with a heart.

JENNY

Our Father who art in heaven,
Jenny walked in front of a train last night,
Hallowed be thy name, thy kingdom come,
She was only thirty-seven,
Thy will be done on earth, as it is in heaven,
You knew what she was going to do, didn't you, Lord?
Give us this day our daily bread,
She had no hope left,
And forgive us our trespasses as we forgive those who
trespass against us.
Jenny is forgiven, isn't she?
Lead us not into temptation,
Lots of us are on the edge of darkness,
And deliver us from evil,
The only strength we have is yours,
For thine is the kingdom,
And she's living there now,
The power and the glory,
She's yours, Lord,
For ever and ever,
Jenny,
Amen.

Diet

It is impossible to over-emphasize the connection between physical well-being and spiritual peace. I'm not, of course, suggesting that one depends upon the other, because many wonderful people have demonstrated great serenity of spirit in the midst of suffering. I'm simply pointing out that a number of people I know (including myself) have discovered that tiredness, too much alcohol, and overeating, to name but three little items, have the effect of dulling one's awareness of spiritual things.

I know someone who felt far from God for years, and made no progress at all until she went on a strict diet and began to like herself again. This is not a moral statement that I'm making – although (forgive me) it becomes one as soon as we see the truth of it, – but a matter of practical living.

I crouch miserably in my hovel of hypocrisy as I write these words. I get very tired. I do enjoy a drink. I expand and contract like a bull-frog's throat.

Read the words that follow, have mercy on me, and I'll have mercy on you.

DIET

expansion was not good business for my body
then I replaced the four sugars in my tea
with sweeteners no after taste eh funny
fat out fibre shovelled in or through
got a shade depressed a little blue
a friend told me alcohol inflates
gave up claret very nearly died
no more boozing nothing fried
full of tuna fish and dates
planned to cheat but then
a miracle I saw my feet
like other better men
fresh air was sweet
and nature smiled
I ran and leapt
soundly slept
happy child
so serene
so lean
a bit
f i t
I
a t e
a bit
a treat
or trophy
had a steak
a titchy cake
a glass of port
a prize I thought
for dieting so well
oh I smiled as I fell
suddenly I wanted chops
wild eyed I hit the shops
syrup jams and lemon cheese
spring into my trolley please
soggy doughnuts filled with jam
come and make me sticky here I am
chocolate fancy and chocolate plain
welcome to the orbit of my face again
crinkly crunkly crunchy fat fried chips
how I do desire to squelch you in my lips
expansion was not good business for my body

Christmas

Here's the scenario.

The angel Pongo appears in your sitting room at midnight on Christmas Eve, and makes the following speech,

'Greetings, highly favoured one. Behold, the Lord has appointed me to bring you news of great joy. Namely, that thou hast built up such a multitude of Brownie points with thy constant do-goodings and such, that he wisheth to offer thee anything that thy heart desireth, even unto a brand new motor or a holiday in the Algarve with bath and all facilities, or, if thou opteth for such, something more useful but less material, if thou getteth my drift.'

'What, you mean like the knowledge that I am following faithfully in the steps of my beloved master?'

'Well, yes, that sort of thing. Most of them tendeth to go for a Porsche, actually, but what you said would go down like a dose of salts in terms of thy future standing with the boss, him being exceedingly big on humility and the like. Suit thyself, but bear in mind that the boss valueth the truth above silver and gold. If thou fancieth a Porsche but asketh for a cold bath and septic boils he will bloweth his stack – take mine word for it.'

So, what would you choose if Pongo asked you?

What would I choose?

Whatever I wanted, eh?

Well, it wouldn't be a Porsche or anything like that. A

Porsche would rust eventually, and then I would wish I'd asked
for the thing I've always wanted – always.
You'll find out what it is at the end of this poem.

CHRISTMAS

Christmas happens anyway – it happened in our house
     today,
It's good! And yet, I have to say, for me there's some-
     thing missing.
It's not that Santa didn't come; he floated past our
     worldly locks,
He drank his sherry, ate his pie, left me a pair of purple
     socks,
And lots of other things.
My daughter gave me half a beetle in a box, a touching
     sacrifice.
There's no significance, I hope, in all the gifts of scent
     and soap,
In mutant ninja turtle shapes!
And who sent exercising tapes?
That isn't very nice.
My son said, 'Dad, I've spent a lot,
A portable word processor.'
I really was excited till I got,
My pencil in a plastic pot.
But there were toys and Garfield mugs
And boxer-shorts and laughs and hugs,
And anyway, they always say, the thought's the thing
     that really counts.
There's something missing, and it isn't here. I'm not
     sure what it is.

The crib confuses me because – I see it as it surely was,
Divine confusion, shepherds visiting the new-born
shepherd,
Mary proud but puzzled, Joseph close, concerned for
her,
And what would tiny babies want with gold and frank-
incense and myrrh?
Why did a million angels fill the sky, like snowflakes
on a starry night?
I guess that no one quite knew what was going on,
Except that something *right* was happening,
And God was saying, and is saying still,
'Here is my son, do with him as you will.
Though you may kill him he will live for you forever
now,
Not lost in rhymes or mimes or special times,
But in the human heart, where revolutions really start,
And struggles in the darkness never seem to cease.
He offered then, he offers now, the only gift you'll ever
want or need,
The possibility of peace.'

Jane Drain

This is the first of five short sketches involving a writer, that you will find scattered through this book. The first one highlights the difficulty of being truthful with a person who appears to have the direct authority of God on her side.

What *do* you reply to someone who says 'The Lord told me ...'?

JANE DRAIN

W = Writer
G = Guest

W: Now, Miss Drain –
G: Call me Jane.
W: Jane Drain – right. Err ... Jane, you wanted to see me to ask advice about writing. Yes?
G: Yes, well you're a writer aren't you?
W: (*Modestly*) Well ... yes, I am.
G: The Lord has given me some poems (*She plonks a huge pile of papers on the table*) and in my quiet time last week he told me that *you* were going to help me get them published.
W: He, err, he's given you a lot, hasn't he?
G: Yes, and you're going to help me get them published.

W: Well, I'm not sure –

G: I get them all over the place.

W: What?

G: Poems. I never know when one's coming. I'll be lying in the bath –

W: (*Warily*) Mmm ...?

G: And one just comes into my head and I have to jump out of the bath, all dripping and unexpected, and run round the house looking for a biro, and when I've found one I put it down quickly.

W: What?

G: The poem. I put it down as quick as I can.

W: When you say the Lord gives you these poems, Jane, do you mean –

G: Here's one I did this morning (*Takes sheet from pile*). It hit me in the shower when I wasn't expecting it. (*Reads*)

When I into the Bible do look
I think to myself what a jolly good book
And there will be considerable joy
For those who do it read, girl or boy
In it we do learn that man a menace is
Disobeying God since not far into Genesis
Why do not we all ask God for his bounties
Whether we hail from Scotland or the home
    counties?
Let us now to God show all due deference
In ways relating to our denominational preference
That way we might avoid a schism,
This was revealed to me in the shower which is a
    bit like baptism.

W: Well! That was ... well!

G: What did you think?

W: Only *you* could have written that, Jane.

G: Which publisher shall we send my poems to, then?

W: Jane, the fact is that poetry, however, err ... good, is just not a selling proposition.

G: Ah, yes, but these poems were given to me by the Lord, so they *will* sell, won't they?

W: Look, Jane –

G: I've written a little poem for you to read when you go out speaking and all that (*Hands him a sheet of paper*).

W: (*Reads disbelievingly*)

> That I do write books there is no doubt
> Of thicknesses varied, some thin, some stout.
> In them I hope that I do capture
> The means by which we'll escape being left behind
>   when it comes to the rapture.

That's – very moving, Jane. Certainly moves me. Tell me, what exactly do you mean when you say that God *gives* you a poem?

G: Well, I'll be lying in the bath, and –

W: No – no. I mean what happens in your head?

G: I dunno – the words just pop into my head and then pop out on to paper. Anyway, which publisher shall –

W: (*Claps hand to head*) Just a minute, Jane! I think it's happening to me. Yes, there's a poem coming through, and I think it's for you. Listen –

> Thank you for writing your poems divine
> They're part of you, so I guess they're mine.
> But frankly, Jane, it would make more sense
> To publish a few at your own expense.

END

Wooden Man

I had a very negative view of Christianity until I went through a stress illness a few years ago. Having been converted at a time when, generally speaking, one was taught that God more or less held his nose as he allowed filthy repentant scum to slip, lizard-like, into his presence, it never really occurred to me that the Creator was bothered about anything but stopping his verminous followers from pursuing their foul, sinful activities. It wasn't until I heard a sermon by John Collins on the subject of Jesus' parable of the sheep and the goats in Matthew, chapter twenty-five, that it began to dawn on me that Jesus is far more interested in what we *do* than what we don't do.

That sermon was a very important step in my journey towards understanding that, actually, God is nice and he likes me.

What follows is an extract from a production called *Coming Home* that I wrote for our local inter-church group. It is about the *positive gospel* of Jesus, and I make no apology for the fact that it ends rather inconclusively.

WOODEN MAN

A: All I can think about is how rotten I am inside. There seem to be so *many* sins. If you get rid of one, another one pops up to take its place. I don't think I'll ever be good enough to do anything really useful for God.

B: Nobody's perfect, y'know.

C: Well, nobody except my friend Donald. He's never committed a sin in his life.

A: There isn't anyone who hasn't done anything wrong – is there?

C: My friend Donald hasn't.
    (*Pause*)

B: He's never done anything wrong? A perfect Christian?

C: My friend Donald – he'll be here in a minute so you can see for yourselves – he has never stolen, never murdered, never committed adultery, never envied, never lusted, never told a single lie, never been guilty of a cowardly act, never hurt anyone, never hit anyone, never hustled, harassed or hated anyone –

A: But surely –

C: Donald has never been greedy, slothful or avaricious, he's never dropped litter, disturbed the peace, driven with excess alcohol in his blood or destroyed other people's property. He's never had a single unkind thought, he holds no grudges, he never gossips, he's never late or lascivious or libellous. He has never caused, continued or condoned conflict of any kind. He never complains, he never blasphemes, he never gets drunk, he never overeats, he worships no false images, he's never mean or menacing or malicious –

B: But isn't that – ?

C: Donald never watches nasty videos, nor does he condemn people who do, he's never judgemental or over-sentimental, or harsh, or unforgiving. He's never sad, mad, bad or (*Hunts for words*) anti-oriental. He never smokes, he never swears, he's never rude, he never stares. Donald has never ever committed a single sin. Oh, and one other thing.

A: What's that?

C: He won't be going to heaven.

(*Pause*)

A: Why not?

B: Because he's not very good company, I should think.

A: No, seriously – why not?

C: (*Disappears and then reappears carrying Donald, a wooden figure*)

A: Because he's made of wood.

B: But you said –

A: You said he was the perfect Christian.

C: No I didn't – you said that. I just told you about all the things he's never done wrong. The trouble with old Donald here (*Pats him*) is that although he's never committed any of the sins I was talking about, he's never done anything else. He can't – he's made of wood. So – (*Looks at A.*)

A: So ...?

C: So, it doesn't matter if you don't do anything wrong for the rest of your life. It won't make you a Christian and it won't get you into heaven.

A: What will then?

C: Now, that's a *very* interesting question ...

Motivation

It's that writer again, only this time it's not Jane Drain he's having trouble with – it's himself. What really motivates him? Why does he do what he does? What a state he's in!

I remember asking a respected friend what he thought about motivation. He pointed out that when Jesus called Zacchaeus down from his tree he only wanted him to go and get the tea under way. He didn't demand an instant change of lifestyle; that came about as a natural progression from obedience. That seems to be the secret really. If you've been given a job to do, then get on and do it, and let God see to the fine-tuning.

Genuine obedience is just as much from the heart as more mushy things.

MOTIVATION

W = Writer
F = Friend

F: Hello, Rodney! You all right?

W: Hello, Viv – mmm, I've got a lot to be thankful for.

F: Oh, bad as that, eh? D'you want to stop rejoicing for a moment and tell me why you're looking so glum?

W: I dunno, Viv, I've been sitting here trying to write,

and I suddenly thought – why am I doing this? (*Taps page*) Who actually wrote this stuff, me or God?

F: Let's have a look. (*Reads*) 'Five pounds of potatoes, two and a half pounds of sprouts, six eggs and a packet of cornflakes.' This is deep stuff, Rodney, I see your problem. Looks like your handwriting though.

W: Not my shopping list, you twit. I'm talking about my books –

F: Oh, sorry. Your books. Right.

W: I mean – *why* do I write books? I say it's for God, but is it? What's it for?

F: Money?

W: Oh come off it, Viv, you're not seriously suggesting that I write about God for cash?

F: What do they pay you in, then – bananas?

W: No, but...

F: You told me the other evening – after your fourth glass of that wine you said was only slightly alcoholic – that you sift through the post every morning looking for cheques and you don't enjoy your breakfast much if there aren't any.

W: That was just the truth – I mean, that was just an exaggeration. You've got me confused now.

F: Maybe it's personal fame and glory, Rodney.

W: Maybe *what* is personal fame and glory, Vivienne?

F: Well, you know, the reason you write. Maybe you write so that people will think you're wonderful?

W: How long have you had this ministry of encouragement, Viv? Here, I didn't say anything about *this* after my fourth glass of wine, did I?

F: No.

W: Oh, good …

F: It was after your fifth –

W: Oh, blimey …

F: You said that, every now and then, you go down to the local Christian bookshop and look in the indexes of the new publications to see if you've been quoted.

W: (*Groans!*) Oh, I didn't say that, did I?

F: Was it true?

W: Well, it wasn't untrue … (*She laughs*) So you don't think there's anything good and pure motivating me to write?

F: I didn't say that.

W: No, but you've taken an interesting, sophisticated problem and reduced it to sordid issues of money and vanity. Blow you, Viv. I was really enjoying my problem till you came along.

F: Look, answer me two questions, Rodney.

W: (*Sulkily*) I don't remember having a sixth glass…

F: No – no, listen! Do you believe God wants you to write books?

W: Well – yes, I do really. Yes, I do, definitely – I think. No, I do! I do think he wants me to write books. Why?

F: (*Holds up shopping list*) Who's going shopping for this lot?

W: What?

F: Who's doing the shopping?

W: (*Shrugs*) Probably send one of the girls down. Is there something wrong with that?

F: No, but hadn't you better check her motivation before she leaves? Have you ever tasted sprouts bought by someone whose motives are mixed? Yuck!

(*Pause*)

W: Viv.

F: Yes?

W: Clear off – I've got some writing to do...

END

Creed

Speaking at a local church a few years ago, I held up a jigsaw puzzle that had been specifically made for the occasion by a friend who is less ham-fisted than I am. It was the normal rectangular shape, but right in the centre of the puzzle was a large, tortuously shaped section that was nevertheless accommodated perfectly by the more orthodox pieces that surrounded it. Each of those surrounding pieces had needed to become a little bit irregular itself, but only on one side. I was making a plea for acceptance and tolerance of individual differences in members of the church community, and suggesting that the doctrinal frame of our faith is quite capable of holding and enclosing people as they are, and not as they should be.

Thank goodness God allows us to be what we are, and enables us to move towards becoming what we should be. We can be honest with him about the shape of our faith, even if it seems a bit irregular at the moment. One of my moments was shaped in the way that this poem describes.

CREED

I cannot say my creed in words.
How should I spell despair, excitement, joy and grief,
Amazement, anger, certainty and unbelief?
What was the grammar of those sleepless nights?

Who the subject, what the object
Of a friend who will not come, or does not come
And then creates his own eccentric, special dawn,
A blinding light that does not blind?
Why do I find you in the secret wordless places
Where I hide from your eternal voice?
I hate you, love you, miss you, need you, wish that you
would go.
And yet I know that long ago you made a fairy-tale
for me
About the day when you would take your sword
And battle through the thicket of the things I have
become.
You'll kiss to life a sleeping beauty waiting for the
prince to come.
Then I will wake and look into your eyes and
understand
And for the first time I will not be dumb
And I shall say my creed in words.

Strength and Vulnerability

The greatest weakness is the fear of being weak.

French proverb

STORIES,
SONGS,
POEMS &
SKETCHES
by Adrian Plass

Strength and Vulnerability

Quite early on in my writing career I was asked to work at an event called 'Take Seven'. (I think this referred to the number of spare tents each family needed to have because the weather was so appalling. Later, this kind of Christian festival became the basis for the section on 'Let God Spring Into Royal Acts of Harvest Growth' in *The Sacred Diary of Adrian Plass*.) Originally I had been asked whether I would be interested in fronting the evening chat-show, but my ideas on how this might develop were not very well received. Unfortunately I was not told this at the time. Instead, it was suggested that I would be much *more* useful in the capacity of seminar speaker on the subject of 'Parenting'. As an inveterate coward of long standing I have every sympathy with the person who curved the truth in this way. He is a charming fellow and I forgive him from the heart of my bottom. Besides, I learned a very valuable lesson down there in Shepton Mallet, as you will see.

Flattered by this implicit trust in my parental expertise, I agreed to address a large group of Christian mums and dads on the subject of bringing up children. It seemed quite easy when I was sitting at home not doing it, but as the date of the festival came closer and closer I began to panic seriously. What could have possessed me to imagine that I had anything remotely useful to say about raising a family? I reviewed my qualifications:

- I had been a child myself; but then, so had everyone else.
- I had been raised by parents. Big deal!
- I had three children of my own, but although I loved and liked them very much the whole business of family had been a Columbus-like voyage of discovery for me. There was no method in my madness.

True, I had dealt with children in care for most of my working life, but such skills as I had acquired in that field seemed to be non-transferable when it came to my own little children's home.

Dismally, I came to the inescapable conclusion that I had nothing to say on a subject concerning which those trusting mothers and fathers would undoubtedly believe I was some kind of expert. How naive I was then! Later, of course, I realized that if a Christian becomes well-known as an expert on – let us say – gardening, he will almost automatically be asked to speak about the theology of fuel injection. You just buy a couple of books, get some notes together, make sure they're heavily laced with relevant verses and Bob's your auntie! Anyone can do it. A lot do. I didn't know that – being so very green.

Then a new and awful thought struck me. My children would be coming along, all three of them, solidly present and visible evidence of the efficacy (or otherwise) of my platform philosophy. A waking nightmare took possession of my mind. There I would be, standing up at the front in a great big leaky tent, lecturing others earnestly on various aspects of fatherhood, when, suddenly, I would become aware that my audience was no longer listening. Instead, their eyes and attention would be fixed on the open tent-flap behind me, through which my offspring would be clearly visible trying to kill each other on the grass outside. Grim-faced, I dismissed the nightmare and gathered my little darlings together. They sat in a row of three as I addressed them thus:

'Listen! Daddy's doing seminars on parenting, right? So I don't want any trouble, Gottit?'

'Yes, yes, yes!' they all said. 'We'll be good, of course we will ...'

The time came, and we set out in our big old green Peugeot tank. The car was stuffed tight with camping equipment, food in cardboard boxes, children, sundry sporting accessories and quite a bit of rubbish from our last major trip. I don't drive. My wife, Bridget, drives. I navigate. My oldest son says this is like asking Cyril Smith to break the world pole-vault record. He's a very silly person sometimes.

The fact that we ran out of petrol fifty yards from the house didn't trouble me too much. After all, Bridget was the captain of the ship, as it were, so we could blame her, and we did.

Some time later, however, things began to get a little more serious. Bridget stopped the car, turned to me as I sat with the map on my knees, and said, 'Adrian, why is the road getting so small? Why are we in a village called Funtington?'

The children had been singing, 'We're off to Shepton Mallet! – we're off to Shepton Mallet!' Now they started to sing, 'We've ended up in Funtington! – we've ended up in Funtington!'

All parents know how angry it is possible to get with children in a car. The vehicle turns into a ghastly red-hot oven full of sub-human fiends whose only talent is torment. I got furious with the children because I felt guilty, Bridget got furious with me because she thought I should be getting furious with myself instead of getting furious with them, and finally I took refuge in a sulk, hoping that by the time I came out of it everyone would have forgotten that it was my fault in the first place.

Whatever the ins and outs of this charming little domestic scene, by the time we arrived in Shepton Mallet the Plass clan was in a BAD state. As we passed through the main gates of the festival showground the lad who was checking tickets enquired in the mildest of tones, 'Are you speaking on something?'

'Yes,' I growled back venomously, 'PARENTING!'

I decided that the best way to restore harmony was to get the tent up, a good communal effort. Yes, you're absolutely right – I know nothing about camping or communal efforts. The strange, recently bought, aggressively heavy slab of canvas that we dragged from the back of our exhausted car bore no resemblance to any tent that I had ever erected. It was like a dead thing that had gone to heaven and didn't want to be bothered with coming to life again. When we did, at last, work out what was meant to go where, it was discovered that Daddy (me) had forgotten to include an essential pole. My family stood round in a circle and stared at me in the same way that people stare at some electrical appliance that has finally gone beyond repair. My oldest son went off and somehow managed to scrounge a spare pole that supported our tent (and our marriage) for the rest of the week. Glumness reigned.

By the time the morning came I was ragged. The thought of standing up in front of all those Christian parents was just too awful to contemplate. If you have ever had to tell people about God immediately after being vile to some close member of your family you'll know exactly what I mean. You want to die, but you can't.

Up I got, clutching a piece of paper on which were listed nineteen wonderfully shiny points about being a good father. I glanced at it before beginning to speak, and silently said to myself, 'Well, you don't do any of them.'

It was then that a little voice seemed to say, 'What about telling the truth?'

'No,' I said to myself, 'we've managed without the truth in the Church for years. Why should I go and spoil it all now?'

But I decided to give it a go. I described to those present the events of the last twenty-four hours. I talked about my bad temper and my sulks. I confessed that the last thing I felt qualified to do was to pontificate about parenting. I thought it might have depressed them, but it didn't. You should have seen their faces brighten! Obviously none of them were very keen on having their mistakes itemized in nineteen easy-to-understand sections! *I* wouldn't have fancied it either. What those people really needed was permission to be vulnerable, and my admission of failure had offered them exactly that. Being a parent can be so painful sometimes. The last thing most of us want or need is to be intimidated by the bright and flawless ones.

That experience at 'Take Seven' was the beginning of an essential understanding that vulnerability is a strength rather than a weakness. That applies just as much to public ministry as it does to selling cabbages. Here comes the second batch.

Worry

Jesus was very hot on 'not worrying', wasn't he? Storms, food, clothing, what to say when the time comes, nasty things that people say about us, death itself – these are just a few of the things we're not to get hot and bothered about. I suppose that if we had the same insight into things of the Spirit that the master had, we would be all too keen to relegate this team of concerns to the foot of our table of priorities.

As it is, many of us are locked into constantly recurring patterns of worry, often about things that are almost certainly never going to happen. It's easy to say we shouldn't be troubled in this way, but how *do* we break these patterns and become free?

As usual (at least I'm consistent) I have no easy answers, only a couple of suggestions.

First, Jesus said that the truth (or 'reality' as it can accurately be translated) will be the thing that sets us free. Perhaps a re-reading of the Gospels, with some sleeve-pulling prayer, will give us new insight into what reality really means. Let's not be silly about this – nobody is going to abandon deeply ingrained habits of worry because someone says it's a bad idea. There has to be a genuine change of perspective and probably a touch of the Spirit before anything radical happens.

Secondly, the 'truth' demands that we look honestly at what our worries actually are. When we have faced them with (possibly) a little more courage than usual, we might talk to another person about them, and that might be the first step towards constructing a plan of escape.

Whole lives are wasted by worry – about the wrong things?

WORRY

No burglars came again last night,
Just as they failed to come the night before
And for as many nights as I remember,
No burglars yet again
Although I listened, as I always do for them,
Once more they did not oil and ease the rusty bolt that
     holds the garden gate
Behind the shed beside the house,
Nor did I hear them moving in the yard at some heart-
     sobbing wretched hour.
It was the ticking of a clock upon my wall
That like the pad of evil steps a hundred feet away.
They did not creep inside,
Their blind-from-birth brutality reduced to stealth and
     whispers
Did not stand above me,
Were not there with threats and ugly promises,
Intoxicated by the scent of fear incontinent
Nor did they then, with weapons that I meekly placed
     into their hands,
Proceed to sever from my chilled insides
The screaming child who has evaded birth for so long
     now.
They did not come.
They were not here again last night
And what if they should never come?

51

A waste of nights – I might have slept
But if I had, I feel quite sure
They would have come, those burglars
Yes, they would have come.

Beams

I wish I didn't have such an appetite for gossip.

'Adrian, there's something I feel I have to say to you about Mavis, but I'm very anxious that you don't feel I'm just spreading stories around for the sake of it. We're both fond of Mavis and I know your only concern will be for her welfare. Are you with me?'

Oh, yes, yes, yes, yes, yes! A thousand times yes! Of course I'm with you, whoever you are. Gimme the dirt on Mavis and we can call it anything you like. I've put my mature, non-judgemental, seriously-concerned expression on, so let's get to it – what's she done, eh?

My wife, who is looking over my shoulder as I write this, has just suggested that I'm being a little hard on myself.

'I agree with most of the negative things you write about yourself,' she says (thank you very much, dear), 'but you've worked hard on this gossip thing. I don't think you do it much any more.'

'Unlike some people we could name, eh?' I reply.

She has left, slightly annoyed.

But Bridget is right, I think. Although the appetite remains, unabated, I have tried to make a habit of countering criticism with praise, and simply not co-operating with muck-spreading ploys. I still fall sometimes, but it hurts me so much when I hear about others doing it to me, that I don't want to do it to anyone else.

As far as the church is concerned gossip is a killer, one of those noxious dark fluids that ooze in to fill the vacuum created by absence of courage, security and reality. I read somewhere once that gossip is a psycho-social necessity. I'm not sure what that is – but I don't agree. It's a bad thing.

BEAMS

A: Just between the three of us
   There's something I should share
   It's in the strictest confidence
   And purely for prayer
   But I just saw young Martin Spence
   With Mrs Falloway
B: You mean they're having an affair?
C: You told us he was gay
A: I think he was until last week
   But now the healing touch
   Has reached him through our loving prayers
C: We must have prayed too much
B: I really like old Martin
A: I think he's great –
B: Me too
A: It's such a shame he's lost control
C: He sometimes has a few
B: But we don't condemn our brother
A: No! As one we sink or swim
   We've all been down that sinful road
C: But not as far as him…
   Hey, Martin, fancy seeing you!
B: Glad you made it, mate!
A: We've been upholding you in prayer

MARTIN: I'll tell you why I'm late.
   I've just been down the hospital
   With Mrs Falloway
A/B/C: Ah!
MARTIN: Her husband's in for treatment
   And she's visiting today
A/B/C/: Oh!
MARTIN: But listen – just in confidence
   And purely for prayer
   You know the place where people wait
   Well, guess who I saw there.
A/B/C/: Who?
MARTIN: Well, who believes that Christian folk
   Should not be sick or ill?
   Who would use a drop of oil
   Where others use a pill?
A: Mildred Smith!
B: A godly lass!
A: Her faith is sure and strong
B: She's full of hope and charity
A: She's good
B: She's kind
C/MARTIN: She's wrong.
A: Ah, Mildred, what a nice surprise!
   You're just in time for prayer
MILDRED: I've just come from the hospital
MARTIN: I know – I saw you there.
A: Something wrong then, Mildred?
B: We're concerned
C: Allay our fears
MILDRED: I visit there on Wednesdays
   I've been doing that for years.
MARTIN: Oh!

MILDRED: But if we're lining up for prayer
     Here's something for the queue...
 A: Is it something confidential?
 B: Is it just between us few?
MILDRED: Yes, the vicar's looking desperate
     That man is never free!
     What with services and visiting...
 C: He never visits *me*.
MILDRED: He told me he's exhausted
     But he doesn't want it known
 A: No!
 B: Of course not!
MARTIN: We'll be very careful
 C: Where's the nearest phone?
 A: Let's pray!
 B: Oh, Lord, protect us!
 C: Don't put us to the test
MARTIN: Forgive us all our trespasses
ALL: As we forgive the rest.

Postmen

If we're going to be all metaphorical now, and it looks as if we are, then I have to say that my wife has been the most important 'postman' in my life.

When Bridget and I did an evening together in the theatre tent at Greenbelt '91, the show was entitled 'Mrs Plass and her husband'.

Bridget came on first and recited the following lines:

Behind the greatest men, they say,
A woman humbly stands,
Her task to serve the genius she wed.
In all my girlish dreams,
I longed to be with such a man,
But then I married Adrian instead.
Perhaps I lack humility,
Perhaps I am too proud,
But if I were to stand behind him here,
The bountiful excess,
With which his stomach is endowed,
Would fill the stage and I would disappear.
The questions get me down,
How's Gerald? Are the Flushpools real?
I like that monk,
Is he a local man?
Exactly why was Leonard Whatsit borrowing the cat?

And how come you're called Bridget, and not Anne?
To those of you who feel
(And there are some of you who might),
That being Mrs Plass should thrill my heart,
He has a ghastly habit,
That would give you quite a fright,
It's –

At this point I made an appearance on stage just in time to cut short the awful revelation. But that bit of nonsense had some truth in it. Bridget has been an immeasurable source of support and strength as far as I'm concerned, and quite apart from putting up with those ghastly habits that she nearly mentioned, she has been the most reliable postman of all in my life, delivering common sense and the heart of God to me on so many occasions.

And now it's time for me to come out of the closet and confess to my post habit. Be strong – it's not a pretty story.

POSTMEN

I have become a post junkie. I can no longer live without my daily fix. Sundays are a nightmare. What will become of me?

It's not even as though I like much of my post when it does come. Bills are nasty, circulars are boring, letters asking why I haven't replied to the last two letters are guilt-inducing, and invitations to come and collect my prize at a local hotel from time-share salesmen drive me into a wild frenzy.

So why do I begin to salivate mentally at eight-thirty each morning? Why do I pace restlessly to and fro by the window of the upstairs sitting-room and gaze yearningly up the road in the direction from which the postman usually comes? Why, when the dog goes berserk and the letter-box clatters, and the mail lands with a muted thump on the front mat, does my heart leap up with joy and anticipation? I suspect that part of the answer lies in the random quality of post – anything could come from anywhere and anyone. It is a regular source of potential unexpectedness in a life which, with four children at school, is necessarily as ordered as people like us can manage.

It is also, as my oldest son would be quick to point out, because I am prone to developing loony obsessions. This same oldest son, knowing how I pant like a thirsty dog for my daily epistolatory dose, will sometimes sprint to the front door before I can get there, scoop up the mail in one well-developed movement, and retreat to his bedroom. There, behind hastily erected barricades, he can enjoy the scratching, whining and bloodthirsty threat-making that emanates from his sad, demented father as he laments for that which he has not got. One day I shall push *him* through the letter-box.

My mania reached new heights at a past address when it began to seem to my feverish imagination that different postmen were bringing different kinds of post. The same part of me knew that this could not possibly be so, of course, but sometimes the evidence appeared to be overwhelming.

There were three postmen.

The first, and most regular one, was a grandfatherly older man with kind eyes and a relaxed, benevolent aura. He pushed a trolley around his 'walk', as

I believe it is called, and he never seemed to be in a hurry. This excellent postman could be relied upon to bring fat cheques, warm letters from old, dearly loved friends, and invitations to dinner parties with people we liked. A Father Christmas of the postal world, he had nothing but goodies in his sack.

The man who regularly brought the second post was a different type altogether. He was very much younger for a start, no more than nineteen or twenty, and he conducted himself with a carelessness that bordered on flippancy. Often, from my post at the upstairs window, as the time for second post approached, I would see this lightweight young person swinging round the corner at the top of our road on his bicycle, and watch as he then pedalled along the straight stretch with his hands off the handlebars and a dreamy smile on his face. I would have laid heavy odds on his being involved with an unskilled but highly ambitious rock band.

The post he brought was pathetic – predictably so. He brought vouchers offering 10p off well-known makes of washing powder; large, impressive-looking envelopes with huge print screaming that you'd probably won £50,000, only you knew you hadn't; unsealed brown envelopes containing the quarterly bulletin of the Retired Gentlefolk's Association and addressed to the person before last who lived in your house. He just didn't try. He wasn't cut out to be a postman.

The third one was the worst of all! He filled in when the older man was ill or on holiday, and I dreaded his coming. Small, thin, horribly clean and unremittingly severe in his manner, he was, we happened to know, a member of the small but very stern religious group that met every Sunday in a little corrugated iron hut at the other end of the town.

During the weeks when he delivered to us, the supply of fat cheques and warm letters simply dried up. I know why – they would have been bad for us. Instead, he brought knife-edged envelopes containing bills that were red with anger, postcards from the public library demanding the return of their books, letters from the bank charging fifteen pounds to point out that we hadn't any money, and ranting communications from members of obscure sects who, having read and disapproved of one of my books, wanted to point out that I would spend an eternity of misery with Satan unless I spent a lifetime of misery with them.

He was a terrible postman!

So what is the point of all this? Well, it's very simple really. I was wrong about the three postmen. It was just a fantasy. They all brought the same selection of post because they were all employed by the same firm. However much I may have wished it otherwise, their character and temperament were irrelevant to the items that they actually delivered.

Sometimes I'm tempted to ignore or discount ministry that's offered to me through an individual or a church that isn't to my taste or liking, especially, in my case, if it's someone who is familiar and close to me.

Let us beware! God sends the messages *and* he runs the entire delivery service. The rest of us are just postmen.

Graces

I was rather pleased when a friend rang to ask if it would be possible for me to write a 'grace' to be said before the meal at a local gathering of Licensed Victuallers. What a pleasure it was to produce something for a group of people who have probably never heard of Graham Kendrick – or Adrian Plass, for that matter.

What a lot of colour and life we miss by avoiding what we suspiciously refer to as 'the world'.

I was severely handicapped, of course, by my profound ignorance of alcoholic drinks, but after much anxious thought I suddenly remembered my friend, Eric Delve, mentioning that he had once had a small port in a public house in Godalming. I hastened to ring him, and to my relief found that he recalled the incident quite clearly. What a memory he has! Even after such a great lapse of time Eric was able to recollect the names of several drinks that had been bought by other patrons of the bar.

Off I went, but after completing the Licensed Victuallers' Grace I got a bit carried away and did one for taxi drivers as well. The mania had me in its grip by the time that one was finished, and I steamed ahead with something suitable for British Rail employees. When my wife came in I looked at her with crazed eyes and held up a list of fifty or more different occupations.

'Look,' I said, 'I'm going to write a grace for every single one, even if it takes – '

'Three's enough, I would think,' said my wife.

Here they are. I'm going to do some more when she's not looking.

GRACES

1) **For Publicans:**
   Lord, we meet together here,
   Mild and bitter, stout and pale.
   Grant, from now till final orders
   That our spirits never ail.
   With specific gravity
   We shall hock depravity,
   Please fill each hungry cavity
   Let gratitude prevail. Amen

2) **For Taxi-Drivers:**
   Simple thanks we offer now,
   No trace of ambiguity,
   For once we'll take this humble fare
   Expecting no gratuity. Amen

3) **For British Rail Employees:**
   Speed this food, Lord, as it comes
   On its journey to our tums.
   Let there be no long diversion
   Of this edible excursion,
   Unavoidably delayed
   Just behind the shoulder-blade,
   Or stranded in the lower back
   By lettuce leaves upon the track.
   May all traffic safely pass
   And our digestions be first-class. Amen

Lewis and I

You may have some difficulty in believing that the little story I'm about to tell you is true. I can understand that, but try to fight this lack of trust within yourself. Above all, please don't get the idea that I'm just cashing in on the Lewis industry as so many other people have done. We Christian writers are not afraid of our personal limitations, you know. Ha! The very thought.

After all, I *might* have met him.

Can you prove I *haven't* met him?

He was alive during my lifetime so I *could* have met him.

Were you there when I *didn't* meet him? (Not that I didn't – I did.)

Anyway, if that's the way you feel, nobody's *making* you read it.

Oh, go on – read it.

LEWIS AND I

I thank God that I am more restrained than other men.

Despite a flood of highly attractive offers from major international publishers I have, until now, refused to describe or discuss the intimate details of my encounter with C. S. Lewis. The memory is sacred to me, and were it not for the specific leading that I have recently felt, I would have quite happily taken my secrets to the grave.

It was, then, on a cold and blustery autumn afternoon in Oxford, as I was in the very act of purchasing a fresh cream doughnut in a small but interesting baker's shop near the centre of town, that I suddenly espied the great thinker and writer standing in the doorway of a shoe-shop on the opposite side of the road.

I was transfixed, as you may imagine, for the entire ninety seconds that elapsed before a car drew up and transported the creator of Narnia away to some other world. Hardly able to believe what had just happened, I took a pen from my pocket and begged a paper bag from the girl who had been serving me. Impressed perhaps by the luminous urgency of my expression, she pushed one into my hand and retreated into some back room or area of the shop.

That paper bag, covered in hastily scribbled notes, lies before me now, evoking memories as fresh as the cream in that distant doughnut, long ago consumed, but never to be forgotten.

Lewis was standing (my notes inform me) with his weight evenly balanced on both feet – and how fitting that was! One foot in fantasy and one foot planted, with exactly equal firmness, in the reality of what *is* and cannot be ignored or changed. It was the balance also between academia and that oh-so-profitable awareness that great truths must be taught with great simplicity by great minds. One would not wish to read over much significance into random events, but it seemed to me that there was what I can only describe as a sort of parabolic synchronicity in Lewis's decision to position himself in front of an establishment that sold footwear. For he himself was responsible through his writings for providing so many folk with the winged sandals, not of Hermes, but of free and unburdened access to the things of God. (It is interesting to note that immediately after Lewis's departure – the shop closed!)

Tears and jam blur a part of my next note, but the picture in my mind is too clear for recollection to fail. Lewis extended his right hand – palm upward – and gazed at the sky for a full five seconds or more.

Yes, the storm clouds were gathering, and yes, the first fragmentary drops of October rain (God's 'natural baptism' as G. K. Chesterton called it) were steadily beginning to fall on that hand whose sure grip had already penned so many and such varied works of literature.

In that moment I seemed to see both a resistance and a submission in Lewis's response to the wild weather of adversity, criticism and self-doubt. He did up one button of his jacket – but *only* one. He frowned slightly towards the clouds, but almost immediately withdrew even further into the shelter of the shop doorway, perhaps seeking in an instinctive way the surrounding comfort of those symbols of individual progress that thronged the windows on both sides of him. From, as it were, the casemented warmth of popular affirmation he would be able to emerge fearlessly (Lewis was *not* carrying an umbrella) into the inclemency of disapproval and difficulty.

Engorged with the richness of these unique insights, my doughnut still untouched, I hardly dared continue to watch as the final act of this fascinating drama began to unfold. Without any warning Lewis lifted his left wrist, cupped his right hand around his watch, and peered intently at it for a second or two before raising his head and nodding, as if to say: 'Yes, it *is* time.'

And, of course, it *was* time. It was Lewis's time. It was my time. It was and is and will be the time of those generations who have and shall and must benefit from the offerings of such a genius. It was with a smile of infinitely sweet sadness that Lewis greeted the arrival of the vehicle he was awaiting, a smile that bade farewell to the *then*, welcome to the *now* and patient resignation to the *not yet*.

It was a privilege to be there on that day, and it surprises me not one iota that responses to the leaking of this unique experience have been uniformly negative. Already an article has been published in America, claiming that Lewis was speaking to an audience of hundreds in a completely different country on the day in question, but that, I fear, is the voice of jealousy braying across the Atlantic.

Next year I plan to publish a paper examining the style and content of a note left by Lewis for his milkman in the late fifties. I believe in my heart that this recently discovered document will establish beyond all reasonable doubt that C. S. Lewis wrestled with an obsessional desire to control the working habits of others.

True scholars could not be other than appreciative.

Angels

know very little about angels. I know that they are God's
messengers – more than messengers. I know that they fight,
and comfort, and protect, and that we might entertain them
unawares.

I know also that they would like the opportunity to become
sons and daughters of God – the opportunity that *we* have.

I wonder if it takes some of them a while to accept their
limitations? Do you think God will forgive me if I undertake a
brief, whimsical conjecture? I hope so, because here it comes.

ANGELS

Two angels were gossiping in the waiting-room of
the buckshot clinic.

'I don't complain,' said the larger one, 'because
I'm an angel, but if I wasn't I'd have something pretty
sharp to say about the allocation of names to us heavenly beings. It's all right if you're called something like
"Gabriel" or "Michael". They've got a real ring to
them.'

'What are you called then?' asked the smaller angel.

'Pongo – that's my name. No wonder I didn't get any
mention in the boss's book. "The angel Pongo appeared
to Mary ..." Doesn't quite have the same impact, does
it? What's your name?'

'Biggles,' replied his companion sadly. 'My name is Biggles – forever.'

Silence descended as the two angels contemplated an eternity of ignominious nomenclature.

'And another thing,' said Pongo, after a minute had passed, 'I was on that angelic sub-committee that was supposed to ratify the boss's plans for his son's visit to the third planet. They gave me that Prodigal Son story to comment on. But did they take any notice of what I said?'

'Well, did they?' enquired Biggles with real interest.

'Did they, heaven! You've seen the final draft. I would have been furious, if I was capable of negative responses. I put in a very full report. Look, I said, the whole thing needs tightening up and refocusing. First of all, there's the road that this prodigal's travelling on. It's so vague! Anyone would think that the boss is willing to travel down any old cart-track that these human wrecks come staggering up once they've realized which side their bread's buttered on. Narrow it down! That's what I recommended. Spell it out! Create an orthodoxy! Pin 'em down!'

'They didn't listen?' Biggles shook his head sympathetically.

'If I was capable of criticism,' said Pongo, 'and the boss was less than perfect, I'd say that this story embodies the kind of flabby liberalism that makes life so difficult for us angels. Why does the father come rushing down towards this wretched son of his while he's still a long way off? It gives the game away – that's what I said in my report. Why not let the kid do the whole trip? Keep him worried and guessing right up to the point where he reaches home. Then leave him standing at the door for a few minutes. Let him stew.

Send the least important serving girl to let him in, and when he does finally get to see his father, let the old man be distant – a little bit cool. The son has to earn his way back into his dad's good books. That's what I suggested.'

'Instead of which ...?' coaxed Biggles.

'Instead of which,' continued the larger angel, 'we have what is (let's be frank) this embarrassing portrayal of the boss going for Olympic gold as he sprints down the highway with a bag of presents, like Father Christmas on jet-propelled roller-skates. Too vulnerable!'

'Too obvious,' nodded Biggles.

'Too easy,' asserted Pongo.

'Too emotional,' added Biggles, rather absently.

'Too generous,' declared Pongo, really enjoying himself now.

'Too wonderful,' said Biggles dreamily.

Pongo frowned and shifted in his seat. 'I might as well have not bothered sending in a report at all,' he muttered. 'Why deliberately provoke those Jewish humans by having the prodigal end up working with the pigs? That's another of the points I made. Then there's the cultural context. What happens, I wanted to know, when we reach the twentieth century, and people start calling it The Parable of the Failed Father? To my mind the boss was laying himself wide open. Two failed kids. Poor parenting. See what I mean? And why so tough on the older brother anyway? Poor bloke, slogging away – doing his best without so much as a thank you. No wonder he wasn't very pleased when his dirty-stop-out brother got all that V.I.P. treatment. If I'd been him I'd have had something to say about – just a minute!'

He looked narrowly at his fellow angel.

'What?' said Biggles, innocently.

'You just said the idea of the boss running down the road was "too wonderful". That is what you said, isn't it?'

'Well,' said Biggles, turning slightly pink, 'I was just thinking that, *if* I was capable of feeling envious, I might have wished that I could walk up the road like the prodigal and see the boss rushing down towards me looking all excited and throwing his arms round me and giving me all those gifts and throwing a party for me and telling me he loved me and – and all that. He's crazy about those humans, isn't he?'

Pongo looked into his companion's shining eyes for a moment, then sighed and smiled a sad little smile.

'Yes,' he said quietly, 'I suppose that if I had been capable of feeling envious, I might have envied ... all that.'

Positive Graffiti

Once or twice people have suggested that I am too negative about life, the Church, and everything. It hurts me to say this, but they may be right. Some good things have happened in my life.

So here, to make the people who've suggested I'm too negative feel good, and to earn me an extra blessing for listening to criticism and acting on it, is – (*Roll of drums*) something positive!!!!

POSITIVE GRAFFITI

I have discussed elsewhere the way in which Satan uses his infernal aerosol spray to cover our hearts with graffiti. Jeremiah said that God will write his law on our hearts, but where these devilish scrawlings are too deep and too numerous to be easily erased, it can be a very long time before the Holy Spirit finally completes the cleaning job and enables us to present a clean sheet to the divine scribe.

Abuse, harsh words, ridicule, failure, rejection – the devil's negative graffiti come in many different forms. Sometimes a few words, not intentionally harmful but thoughtless and ill-chosen, can cause a wound that takes years to heal, and leaves a scar that never quite fades. How dangerous the tongue is!

It occurred to me recently, though, that, in my own life at any rate, there have been correspondingly positive experiences, events and influences that have counteracted or even replaced some of the negative ones. These heavenly graffiti come in many different forms, often through agents who have no specifically Christian connection. They are little gifts from God that may have a disproportionately profound effect.

I can remember three without really trying.

The first happened when I was about five years old and attending the little infants school in the village of Rusthall, where I was brought up. I was a slightly worried child, not particularly naughty, but given to occasional outbursts when I felt driven into a corner. One day I did something naughty in the playground, halfway through the dinner hour. I can't remember exactly what it was that I did but I do recall my awareness that it was 'a fair cop'. I was for it! The lady who was on playground duty dragged me into the top classroom and left me there while she reported my crime to the headmistress. When she came back she told me I was to wait on my own until the head sent for me.

I was terrified. My hair stood up and my blood drained down. What tigers there were in this jungle of a world!

At last the headmistress appeared at the classroom door and beckoned me to follow her through the corridor and into her office. I stood facing her as she sat behind her desk. I felt my bowels move ominously. What was going to happen?

After a moment's silence the headmistress pointed to a bowl on her desk and said, 'Come and sit down and have some ice-cream Adrian.'

She picked up a second bowl, and we sat, side by side, eating ice-cream together. She never mentioned my dreadful misdemeanour, and I certainly wasn't going to bring it up. I didn't feel any satisfaction about 'getting away with it'. I was just puzzled and surprised and relieved to find that authority did not exclude mercy.

The second experience happened just outside Paddington Station in London. I was a raw, unsophisticated teenager, anxious to project a cool, confident image to the rest of the world. A porter carried my bags from the train on which I'd travelled, to the bus-stop just up the road from the station. As he bent down to put my luggage on to the pavement I felt in my pocket for some change. I knew what to do now. When porters carried your bags you gave them a tip. How much? I didn't know – I'd never been in this position before.

Withdrawing my hand from my pocket I looked at the selection of coins. Airily I selected two florins (a florin was the same as a ten pence piece) and handed them to the porter, who was just straightening up. He stood quite still for a second or two, studying the two coins that lay in the palm of his hand, then, after a searching look into my face, he handed one of them back to me, and said, in a voice tinged with some mid-European accent, 'Two shillings is quite enough.'

Even I, naive as I was, knew how unusual it was for *anyone* to return any part of a tip. The porter had given me a little free lesson. It warmed my heart to know that his generosity extended to strangers. Perhaps he had a son of my age.

Thirdly, there was George.

George worked in a paint distribution warehouse near Bromley, a place where five or six employees plodded around behind metal trolleys, assembling orders to be delivered to retailers. It was a place of long alleys running between high shelving units, loaded with every conceivable variety of paint, a veritable maze.

George was not in love with his work; there was nothing very inspiring about piling tins on trolleys. In his mid-forties and totally lacking in ambition, George was an expert in the art of disappearance. He knew the alleys like the back of his hand, and he spent the day playing hide and seek with the foreman, a little, frantic man with no top teeth who ran around the warehouse clutching a sheaf of overdue orders in his hand, and plaintively calling for one of the mole-like trolley-pushers to come and fill them. Occasionally George allowed himself to be spotted in the distance, passing across the far end of an alley, moving with considerable speed, and looking as if he had suddenly remembered where some obscure variety of paint was stored. George was a master of the art of doing nothing, and he did it all day.

I was working in the warehouse as a vacation job in between terms at the teacher-training college in Bromley. I was in my mid-twenties at the time. Unlike George, I worked very hard at assembling orders, mainly because it was so excruciatingly boring if I didn't. George and I got on very well, though, and one day he saved me from death by tedium.

At that time I was a fairly heavy smoker. It was one of the few things that made life in the warehouse bearable. One day I left my packet at home and was quite desolate. With no money to buy any more I steeled myself to an eternal, cigarette-less day.

George, also a smoker, realized my predicament, and throughout that day, found me at regular intervals, handed me a cigarette without speaking, and returned to whichever bolt-hole he was occupying at the time.

Leaving aside the rights and wrongs of smoking, it struck me then, and it strikes me now, that George, with his redundant teddy-boy haircut, and his rather grey aimless view of life, did a very sweet thing for a fellow human being on that day.

My headmistress, the porter from Paddington Station and generous George, each offered me, in their own way, the cup of water that Jesus talked about his followers needing. And each will undoubtedly receive the reward that he also mentioned.

Thank God for positive graffiti, and those whom he uses to provide them.

You, Me and Us

There is little less trouble in governing a private family than a whole kingdom.

Michael de Montaigne (*Essays*, 1580)

If you wish to study men you must not neglect to mix with the society of children.

Ibid.

STORIES, SONGS, POEMS & SKETCHES by Adrian Plass

You, Me and Us

A few years ago we enjoyed a family holiday in Denmark, and I can testify that there's a lot more to that ancient kingdom than bacon and Lego. The eastern peninsula that we explored was beautiful to look at and full of interest. More importantly from the point of view of our three boys, there was a football pitch and two practice goals just up the road from our holiday house in the village of Stenvad. It was a comfortable place to stay, with a 'cricket-sized' garden at the back.

We had some very silly jokes from some members of the family. Worst of all was the suggestion that when we got home we should take our films into the chemist, then when we returned to collect them a few days later, we would say, 'May we have Hamlet, please?'

'Hamlet?' the shop assistant would enquire.

'Yes,' we would reply, 'the prints of Denmark.'

Gettit?

The best thing, as usual, was just being together as a family, arguing in peace for once.

Sometimes the holiday ethos allows quite subtle problems to rise to the surface.

One evening, after the younger members of the family had finally been coaxed, threatened and bribed to bed, my oldest son put into words an area of concern that had never occurred to me. He described how, as he listened to Bridget and me talking to the younger children, praising them for things they'd said or bought or done, he recognized in the words we used and the tone of our voices, the same kind of encouragement that had enabled him to feel valued and approved of as *he* grew up. Now, however, seeing how positive we were about quite small efforts and achievements on the part of the little ones, he started to feel a little insecure. Perhaps we had been less than sincere when we praised *him* in the past. What if his feelings of allrightness were based on a series of half-truths? Maybe we weren't really proud of him after all.

I didn't really know what to say in reply to this, but by the next morning the issue had resolved itself into a question in my mind: Which is more important in relationships – the love of truth, or the truth of love?

Should our response to the efforts of others be doggedly, uncompromisingly accurate, or should we let love mould and modify our reactions.

I tried to explain what I was thinking to my son, but it was only when I got down to concrete examples in his own life that he began to see what I meant.

'What about you with Katy?' I said (Katy was three and her biggest brother was potty about her). 'What about when Katy brings you one of her drawings and asks what you think of it? Do you say, "I'm sorry, Kate, but it's just a meaningless scribble"? Or do you say, "Well done, Katy, that's really lovely!"? In fact,' I went on, seeing his face soften, 'would you be happy if you knew that the way I feel about you is the same as the way you feel about Katy?'

'Yes,' he said. 'I would.'

'That's good then,' I said, 'because it is.'

The maintenance and repair of relationships with God, family, neighbours and fellow believers is an absolute priority in our lives, but what a tricky area this can be. I was about to say that this next cart-load of 'cabbages' includes some ideas and issues that are rather personal to me, but I think I can safely say that most of us ratbags can easily identify with each other's problems.

So stay with me (unless your relationships are totally under control, of course).

Generations

G. K. Chesterton described atheism as a nightmare – a maze without an exit.

My own atheistic nightmare is concerned with the inexorable roll of the generations. So much birth and death and joy and grief, happening over and over and over like a constantly repeated film, in which only the faces change slightly each time. Grandparents who will probably never know their great-grandchildren, and will certainly never know their great-great-grandchildren, and wouldn't be able to remember all their names anyway because there would be far too many of them.

'Oh, God, let it all mean something!' I have cried at those times when the darkness just won't go away. My heart would break if I ever seriously believed that all our relationships turn to dust. What would be the point of anything?

'Don't be afraid,' said Jesus, 'I have overcome death.'

GENERATIONS

1) I took my daughter to the park last night
   She ran with a shout to the roundabout
   The roundabout went round and round
   But it never stopped anywhere very profound
   It just went round and round and round,
   It just went round and round.

2) I took my daughter to the park last night
   She bounced like a spring to the grown-up swing
   It swung quite high and it swung quite low
   But there wasn't any doubt where the swing would go
   It just swung high and it just swung low,
   It just swung high and low.

3) I took my daughter to the park last night
   Her eyes grew wide when she saw the slide
   She climbed up the steps and she slid back down
   But the same sun set on the same old town
   She just climbed up and she just slid down
   Just climbed and slid back down.

4) We're all going down to the park tonight
   Where the swings go high and the swings go low
   But there isn't any doubt where the swings will go
   And you climb the steps and you slide back down
   While the same sun sets on the same old town
   Where the roundabout just goes round and round.
   And never stops anywhere very profound
   It just goes round and round and round,
   It just goes round and round.

Waste of Days

Our writer is in an even trickier position now than he was before. Having sorted out the abominable Jane Drain, and worked out where he stands on motivation, he is now dead and about to discover if the words he wrote so easily in life will do him any good at the gates of Paradise.

I suspect, although never having been dead I can't be sure, that God's idea of priorities may turn out to be very different from ours. Poor old Rodney Fuller finds that the books he's written are of far less importance than the way he has treated his family, especially in his use of time.

Recently I have become very conscious of the richness of days that most of us possess. So many mornings and after-noons and evenings to use as we wish. We can squander them or spend them wisely, and of course that will mean different things to different people. Walking on the Downs could be the best or the worst way to use a day; helping a neighbour can be selfish or unselfish; working without a break can be admirable or cruel. Our hearts tell us the truth if we want to listen.

Which reminds me – I said I'd go and play snooker with my son this evening.

WASTE OF DAYS

W = Writer
A = Angel

W: (*Approaching desk*) Err ... excuse me.

A: (*Brisk and pleasant*) Yes, sir?

W: Is this ... heaven?

A: Front-desk, yes, sir. Did you want to come in?

W: Well, err, I'm a writer.

A: That doesn't automatically disqualify you, sir. We've admitted publishers before now. If I can just have your name.

W: My name's Rodney Fuller. (*No response*) I wrote Christian books. I've written lots of, err ... Christian books. Are you an angel?

A: Yes, sir, I am an angel.

W: Well, I wrote a book about angels – a sort of novel – you know, about how things really are for angels.

A: (*Dryly staring*) Yes. I read it.

W: And I wrote another book called *Boldness before God: The Certainty of Salvation*. Err ... do you think I *will* be allowed in?

A: I have your file here, Mister Fuller (*Studies it for a moment*), and all your books. (*Puts pile on desk*) These are all yours, are they not?

W: (*Encouraged*) Yes, yes they are. Writing was my ministry, you know.

A: Writing was your *obsession*, Mister Fuller. According to this file you robbed your family, your friends, your community and your church of a year and a half's worth of free time just so that *this* (*Holds up*

book) could be written, for instance. (*Reads title*)
A *Study of the Relationship between Hair-length and Heroism in the Pentateuch.*

W: That was described as 'A very important book'.

A: Yes ... (*Consults file*) by the Latvian Christian Barbers in Exile Association's five-yearly news bulletin, which was only produced once because its seventeen subscribers had all died before the second edition was due.

W: Well, it was a bit of a minority –

A: And while you laboured away on behalf of seventeen octogenarian hairdressers your wife was putting the kids to bed, looking after visitors, cleaning the house, sorting out the bills, fending off door-to-door Spring Harvest salesmen, apologizing to needy people in the local community for your non-availability, writing an article about not having time to write a book, doing a part-time job, mowing the lawn, planting out vegetables, and putting up with your chronic bad temper – all because you had convinced her that you were engaged in the Lord's work!

W: I was committed!

A: You were fanatical.

W: I was creatively absorbed!

A: You were self-indulgent.

W: I was spiritually driven!

A: You were an Anglican.

W: But I thought –

A: Mister Fuller, at birth your account was credited with sixty-nine years, three months and nine days. That is a very sizeable deposit. It has now been spent to the very last moment, and these records suggest that a large proportion of what you used to describe as your 'writing career' involved the squandering of very valuable hours. Balance, Mister Fuller – that is what you failed to achieve – balance!

W: I'm not going to be saved by works, am I?

A: (*Pats books*) Well, not these, no. Up here, Mister Fuller, it's not what you've done or what you know, it's *who* you know.

W: (*Brightening*) I had tea with Eric Delve once.

A: I thought you *wanted* to come in.

W: I do, I was only joking. I – I know Jesus. I've written about him.

A: Oh! (*Examines file – pauses*) Well, let's hope he's written about you...

END

Today's News

I very rarely set out to be obscure in my writing. On the contrary, I can't understand why, in the vast majority of cases, writers would *not* want readers to know what they are getting at. I have to confess, however, that in the following lines, which are song lyrics, the images employed are quite deliberately selected with a view to offering the listener an impression of what I want to say, rather than a clear picture.

Why?

Good question. I suppose the answer is partly that I just enjoyed the freedom of communicating without accountability, and partly that fuzzy pictures can sometimes reveal more soul than photographs.

Having said that, some of the metaphors are quite obvious, and I promise that they all mean *something*. For instance:

For her memory is blind
To the one who touched her body
In the middle of her mind.

This refers to child abuse, and the psychological mechanism that conceals painful memories from the conscious mind, but is unable to prevent the wounds caused by those forgotten events from festering, and poisoning the victim for years.

Can you work out what all the other images are about? Can you be bothered?

The general theme of the piece is that large-scale convictions, movements and principles, even if held and supported sincerely, are not much use if they never affect anything or anybody on a small scale. At least, I *think* that's what it was about...

TODAY'S NEWS

Today's news came on the wrong day
And the right day never comes
Though the man who is tied to the dragon
May smile as he does his sums
But he doesn't understand
That we just can't handle
The pain in the universe.
Someone'd better tell the man, he doesn't seem to care
If love's not down in the market square
It's not anywhere.
It's not anywhere.

The bear is called a pussycat
The cat's become a mouse
But it hasn't made a difference
To the feeling in our house
For mother's in the same old place
The baby's out the back
My brother hit the ceiling
Then he bounced into the crack
And the sun is getting hotter
And the sky is getting old
But the central heating's busted
So our feet are just as cold
It's not that we don't see the dead
A thousand years away

But there's someone in our upstairs room
Who might be dead today

Today's news came ... etc

Would-be-good, the watcher
Wanted poetry in stone
But the valley of the dwellers
Is already overgrown
By the pestilence upon her
For her memory is blind
To the one who touched her body
In the middle of her mind
The icemen love experiments
But this will never do
For the maze is getting difficult
The rats are coming through
And the voluntary patient
Hates the pattern that he's known
For the shape of it is uglier
Than anything in stone

Today's news came ... etc

Somewhere there's a city
Where the washing powder's been
All the citizens are sleepy
And defiantly unclean
But in the solid cells
Behind another city wall
There are people who are clean and grey
And never seen at all
Fifty million babies
Have been planted on the moon
And another stepping-stone

Will be a mausoleum soon
But here we step more warily
Across the wild park
For the city's getting dangerous
The city's getting dark

Today's news came on the wrong day
And the right day never comes
Though the man who is tied to the dragon
May smile as he does his sums
But he doesn't understand
That we just can't handle
The pain in the universe
Someone had better tell the man, he doesn't seem to
    care
If love's not down in the market square
It's not anywhere,
It's not anywhere

Clay

One of the wonderful things about Christian marriage is that you never have any rows or arguments, so when I wanted to write about conflict in relationships I had to go round all my friends asking them if they could tell me what it was like. At last I found some people who remembered having an argument some years ago, and they have kindly allowed me to record the details of that event in this book.

And if you believe all that, you'll believe anything!

Arguments in marriage are like pieces of music – harsh music perhaps, but with familiar and oft-repeated tunes. It seems to me a legitimate function of drama that it should face people with the truth of what they do to each other. Maybe it might even help them to change the music – something a little more harmonious, perhaps?

We must be careful with each other. We are only clay.

CLAY

W: Well?

M: Well what?

W: Aren't you going to ask me how I got on?

M: How did you get on?

W: Well, don't sound too interested, will you? (*Pause*) What's the matter?

M: Nothing. Why?

W: I dunno, you just seem ... funny.

M: How did you get on?

W: (*Excited*) I actually made a pot! I made one! It weighs about three and a half pounds, and it only holds about a thimbleful of water, but it's a pot! My pot!

M: (*Dully*) I thought you didn't go on the wheel for the first few lessons, or have I got it wrong?

W: No, we don't.

M: Oh, don't we?

W: I made this one with my hands, just, you know, squeezing and shaping. It was quite sensual!

M: It was what?

W: The feel of the clay – it's lovely stuff to handle – all squishy and thick and soft.

M: I thought the idea was to acquire a practical skill, not to have sensual experiences.

W: Oh, don't be so grumpy, darling. You're not jealous of a lump of clay, are you? (*Imitates him*). 'I thought the idea was to acquire a practical skill, not to have a sensual experience ...'

M: I don't think doing impressions of me is particularly helpful, do you?

W: What *is* the matter with you? (*Pause*) Have you not had a very good evening? (*Waits*) Michael?

M: I've just been here. Haven't really...

W: I thought you'd enjoy being on your own for a while. Was the dinner all right? (*Pause*) You have had your dinner, haven't you?

M: I couldn't work out the thingy ... I dunno, I just couldn't be bothered in the end.

W: (*Genuinely distressed*) Michael, that was a lovely

dinner! I spent ages getting it ready. All you had to do was turn it up for half an hour then take it out. What do you mean you don't know how to do it? – you've done it loads of times! Why didn't you –

M: Look, I didn't have my dinner, all right! It's hardly the crime of the century, is it?

W: No, but it's meant to punish the crime of the century, isn't it?

M: Don't be stupid! I –

W: The only thing is, we're not quite sure what the crime of the century is, are we? At least, I'm not! Is it my torrid affair with a piece of clay, or is it just that I left you alone to wrestle with the terrible complexity of an oven switch? Or is it something else?

M: (*Strategic sigh*) I'm beginning to wish I hadn't said anything at all.

W: I'm sure you are. Because you haven't actually got any real grievance at all, have you? I thought we left all this sort of stuff behind ten years ago. I just couldn't *stand* it if –

M: (*Overwhelmed*) Look, can we just forget about it now please? I'm sorry! I wish I'd never – I mean – I'm sorry!

W: (*Pause*) Do you want to hear any more about my pot?

M: (*Back in the driving seat*) Yes, go on.

W: Well, it's brown.

M: Mmm … (*Nods*)

W: And ugly.

M: Mmm … (*Nods*)

W: Like you…

M: Humph!

W: (*Quietly*) Especially when you get like you got just now. What was going on? Please tell me.

M: There's no point in telling you.

W: Why not?

M: Because you don't really want to know. It's irrational, and you don't like that. If I tell you what I feel you'll just tell me how wrong I am to feel it.

W: No I won't.

M: Yes you will. You always do.

W: Well, I won't this time. (*Pause*) Try me.

M: (*Unconvinced!*) All right – I feel hurt and upset and threatened by you going out and doing something that doesn't involve me, and being all bright and happy about it and talking about – sensual clay, and ... well, that's about it really.

W: (*Shaking head*) How can you *possibly* feel that?

M: See what I mean?

W: I mean – I just don't understand how you can say that. We *talked* about me doing an evening class. You said you thought it was a good idea. You were the one who persuaded me to get on and actually do it. Now you're spoiling it!

M: Look, you asked me what I was feeling so I told you. I said you wouldn't like it because it's irrational. It *is* irrational! I know it's irrational. But I'm stuck with being who I am and what I am because of all the – stuff in my past and all that. I didn't choose to feel what I felt this evening; it was just there. If you hadn't asked me what was the matter, I wouldn't have told you, then we wouldn't have had a problem would we?

W: (*Temporarily conned*) I'm sorry, Michael. I didn't mean to stir things up. I was just upset that you

95

felt – (*Pause*) Wait a minute! What am I talking about? It's just like the old days. I've ended up apologizing for what you've done to *me*!

M: What?

W: Well, you say we wouldn't have had a problem if I hadn't asked you what was wrong, but that's not true, is it? You were in your 'Guess what's the matter with me' mode from the moment I walked through the door. All morose and moody and (*Whines*) 'couldn't work the thingy on the oven so I didn't have any dinner'. Poor little boy!

It's true, isn't it? You were determined to show me how miserable you were. Tell me the truth for once!

M: (*Apparently deeply hurt and offended*) Are you saying that I usually tell lies?

W: Oh, dear! Have I exaggerated? I do apologize. What a convenient thing to latch on to. We're not *talking* about *my* exaggeration. We're talking about you! When I first met you, you'd just emerged into the adult world with 'A' Levels in sulking, self-pity and – (*Searches for a word*)

M: You can't think of a third word beginning with the same letter, can you?

W: I warn you, Michael! I'm not going back to all that. If I can't do things on my own without you trying to punish me every time...

M: Yes?

W: (*Quietly*) I don't know. (*Pause*) I'm going out. I can't stay here at the moment.

M: Where are you –

W: I don't know where I'm going. I've got my pot in

the boot. I might go down to Brighton for a dirty weekend.

M: Don't be silly...

W: What, irrational, you mean? Well, I'm sorry, Michael, but it's all because of my dreadful past. I'm stuck with being who I am, you see, and you don't have to make any effort to control yourself. I thought you knew that. It's just unfortunate if it affects anyone else. Ring round the hotels if you want to find me. Just ask for Mrs Clay (*Pause*) Oh!! I'll see you later! (*Exits*)

M: Hmm ... (*Longish pause for thought*) I think I'll have some dinner...

(*Blackout*)

I Know What
You're Going to Say

STORIES,
SONGS,
POEMS &
SKETCHES
by Adrian Plass

I Know What You're Going to Say

It's dangerous to assume that we know all there is to know about a close friend or marriage partner. I once acted in a play featuring a married couple who disagreed about the type of house they occupied. She was convinced that they lived in a two-storey house, while he was adamant that it was a bungalow. He had refused to go upstairs for years, because it would prove her point.

This deliberately absurd situation amusingly highlighted the stagnation that can occur when long-term relationships are reduced to a set of predictable, constantly repeated verbal and behavioural shapes. Whole chunks of personality are put into cold-storage because they never became part of the relationship pattern at an early stage.

I always find it so sad to see a couple sitting in a cafe or restaurant, especially on holiday, gazing blankly into the distance because there's no point in trying to communicate when you know exactly how your partner is going to respond. Yes, I know it's a good thing to be able to sit in companionable silence, and no, Bridget and I *don't* always talk animatedly in cafes and hold Wildean conversations in restaurants, but you know what I mean. So sad.

One of the ways in which I annoy Bridget is by suddenly saying, apropos of nothing: 'Who are you?'

I do put it on a bit, but that occasional question is born out of the sudden, genuine realization that this person who is so close to me that I can hardly see her, is actually a quite separate, complex, total human being who I don't know half as well as I think I do. I find those moments rather exciting in a number of ways.

Heaven preserve my relationship with my wife, and with God, from the illusion that I can be totally sure what either of them is going to say.

I KNOW WHAT YOU'RE GOING TO SAY

WOMAN: John, I've been thinking.

MAN: Mmm?

WOMAN: I've made a decision.

MAN: Uh-huh?

WOMAN: I'm going to stop work in September.

MAN: Well –

WOMAN: I know what you're going to say. How are we going to manage on one salary? Well we did it before and we'll do it again. We're far too extravagant anyway. It'll do us good.

MAN: I –

WOMAN: It's no good coming out with that old line about 'How are you going to manage without your holidays and little treats?' It really infuriates me when you say that. You're virtually accusing me of being a simple-minded bimbo, which, for your information, I certainly am not!

MAN: You –

WOMAN: Don't bother telling me I've got some secret reason for stopping work, either. I haven't, and,

102

quite frankly, I take exception to your view of me as a devious, self-seeking female.

MAN: Could we –

WOMAN: No, don't try to smooth me over. You can't call someone a neurotic simpleton and then make it all right with a few glib phrases. No doubt you'll claim you 'didn't mean it'. Well, if you didn't mean it you shouldn't have said it! How would you feel if you'd come to me with a carefully thought through plan and just had it steamrollered? Because that's what you've done.

MAN: I –

WOMAN: No, please don't insult my intelligence by denying it, because I simply won't listen. You've had your say and now it's my turn! Or perhaps I don't get a turn. Well, I'm going to take it anyway. I've told you I want to stop work, but you didn't seem to hear me. Or rather, you did hear me, but all you could do was go on in your usual style about holidays and treats and not being able to manage. So negative as usual! You don't agree with me, so that's the end of that.

MAN: It's –

WOMAN: You don't have to say any more. I get the message. Well, all right – I *won't* stop work! But just you bear in mind that it was you who bullied me into carrying on.

MAN: When –

WOMAN: It's useless trying to back-track now. It's too late! You've got your own way, now you can live with it. Keep on slaving away! Those are your orders to the resident servant. Well, okay, I will. But I loathe you sometimes, and one day I'll find

the words to tell you how much – if I ever get a
word in edgeways, which is unlikely.

MAN: But –

WOMAN: I'm sorry, I don't want to hear any more. You
may not have finished, but I have! I'm going out.
Goodnight! (*Exit*)

MAN: If only I'd kept my mouth shut ...

Navigation

Having undertaken to do a seminar on 'Sex' at Greenbelt '91, I began to lose my nerve. What on earth was I going to say on this thorny subject? 'Parenting' had been bad enough at Take Seven a few years previously, but Sex?

'I'll have to call in sick,' I said to my wife, 'I don't know what to say. I can't come out with all that old 'God created sex – it's a beautiful thing – but only within the context of marriage' stuff. It may be true but it's hardly original, is it? What am I going to do?'

'Calm down,' said Bridget, 'I'll think of something.'

And she did.

'What is it,' she asked a little later, 'that we've had more rows about than anything else while we've been married?'

I went through a list of five or six things that it might have been, but they were all wrong.

'Come on!' said Bridget, 'think hard. What is it that's brought us nearer to physical conflict than anything else?'

And then it clicked. Of course! How could I have been so slow? There was absolutely no doubt about the cause of our most virulent arguments.

MAP READING.

And not just us. I have got into a car before now with the most saintly couple you could hope to meet. Never heard so much as a raised voice from either of them. Then it begins.

'*Why* didn't you tell me there was a turning coming up?'

'Well, last time I told you there was a turning you got cross with me and said you didn't need to hear about every little wrinkle on the map!'

'For your information, that 'little wrinkle' we just missed was our last opportunity to leave this road for the next thirty miles. Thank you very much, I *don't* think!'

'How you can be so unreasonable, I just don't know!' (*She cries*)

And so on, and so on...

'The thing is,' said Bridget, 'that vicars and curates and elders and ministers and people like that ought to counsel engaged couples on map reading. The sex would follow on naturally from that.'

'Err ... the seminar, Bridget?'

'Yes, well what you need to do is write a sketch that combines sex and map reading. We'll start the seminar with that.'

So I did – and here it is.

NAVIGATION

VICAR: Well, now, Sally and Slim, this is the last of our marriage preparation sessions. We've already covered an awful lot of ground –

SALLY: Metaphorically.

VICAR: Yes, metaphorically, we've already covered an awful lot of ground. Last week Slim shared with us that he couldn't actually recall asking you to marry him, Sally, and that he was profoundly horrified by the prospect of spending the rest of his life with you, to the extent that (and I think he put it rather picturesquely) he would rather be stung slowly to death by killer bees than face you over

the breakfast table every morning for the next fifty years. And I think we sorted that one out okay last Thursday. One of those little worries that needs to be aired, and err ... well done, you, for airing it.
Now, your turn this week, Sally, to throw up –

SALLY: Not literally?

VICAR: Not literally, no ... err, your turn to throw up any little last-minute worries or problems.
(*Pause*)

SALLY: Well, there was one thing, and – well it ruined my parents' marriage, so I wondered if we could talk about it.

VICAR: Of course we can, Sally. What is it? (*Pause*) Is it err ... alcoholism?

SALLY: No.

VICAR: Err ... finance?

SALLY: No.

VICAR: Exegetical incongruity?

SALLY: No, we sorted that out with a pair of curling tongs.

VICAR: Ah! So you're talking about –

SALLY: Yes, navigation.

VICAR: Yes, indeed, and I can tell you, Sally and Slim, that many marriages founder on the rock of navigational ignorance and conflict. Something that should be a natural and joyful experience can so easily end in trouble and tears.

SALLY: (*Tentatively*) We were wondering about (*Pause*) positions...

VICAR: Yes, well, traditionally the man – that would be you in this case, Slim –

SALLY: (*Taking out pencil and notebook*) Can I just make a note of that ...?

VICAR: Traditionally, the man would sit in the driving seat, while the woman would sit in the passenger seat with the ... map ... on her knees. Nowadays, many couples prefer to do it the other way round, and there's absolutely nothing wrong with that. As long as both partners are comfortable and happy with what's happening, that's all that really matters.

SALLY: We're going to Leeds for our honeymoon in the car. Do you think we ought to navigate our way up there beforehand, just to see if we can manage it all right?

VICAR: I'm going to say the same thing to you as I say to all young engaged couples. It's perfectly proper to make short trips and excursions in the general direction of Leeds, but I must counsel you against going all the way at this stage. I think Milton Keynes is quite far enough. And once you get as far as Nottingham it's very hard to stop.

Times have changed, of course, since I was a young man. When I was driving out with a young lady it would never have occurred to me to leave Littlehampton, let alone attempt to navigate all the way to Leeds. Not that I wasn't interested, I hasten to add. I well remember getting a terrible roasting from my father when he found a street map of Huddersfield hidden under my mattress.

Now, any other little questions or problems? Once you're married you'll gradually get to know each other's needs and it won't be long before you're reaching your mutual destination very harmoniously on every single occasion.

SALLY. We wanted to ask if it's possible when we

actually start navigating to Leeds – I mean – if we get stuck at a junction, and Slim says it's my fault for reading the map wrong, and I say it's Slim's fault because he wasn't sensitive to the road signs, and Slim says he wishes he'd never married me in the first place, and I hit Slim with the emergency flashlamp that we've asked Uncle Vernon and Auntie Grace to buy us for a wedding present, and we crash because Slim temporarily loses consciousness, and we're on the verge of giving up navigation altogether ...

VICAR: Yes?

SALLY: Well, can you help us then?

VICAR: No, but I know a man who can, and he drives a patrol car in the sky.

SALLY: Literally?

VICAR: Err ... no, metaphorically.

SALLY: Thank you, Vicar. You're a very nice man. You're a very, *very* nice man...

Dear Family

Oone of the pointless questions I ask myself from time to time is whether I would opt for mental or physical pain if I had to choose. It's difficult, isn't it – until you start to live through one or the other, that is. Then you know for sure that you would choose the kind of suffering that you are not being afflicted with.

My own experience has been that, for years, I was quite sure nothing could be worse than extreme physical pain. After all, you can always find a way to distract yourself from mental anguish. That's what I believed, and for most of my early life it was true.

Then I had a family. They have brought me much joy, but also the discovery of a new kind of pain; something to do with observing the gradual death of innocence; even more, I think, to do with my own shortcomings as a father and a husband. Being a morbid beggar by nature I've always made a bit of a meal of these things, but I have known excruciating pain at times, and I've lost the knack of distracting myself.

I'm sure that if I suddenly developed a chronically painful illness, I would long for those good old days of mental torment, but I still can't quite answer that original silly question of mind.

I do feel sorry for Jesus at Gethsemane.

FAMILY

Dear family, I write to you in this campfire place
Where temporary flames repel the savage things
Whose glowing, hungry eyes appear from time to time.
They know, as I do, that a campfire only burns as long
  as fuel lasts.
My stocks are low as ever, and these devils never rest.
But I have light and time enough to write to you
Dear family, asleep, for once, beside me here in peace,
To say how I regret the need to share such fearful trav-
  elling with you.
I know that monster-ridden darkness is my own affair
I have no right to take you there.
The battle I shall face tonight will threaten you
But certainly it never was your fight.
God knows I wish that it was otherwise
That we could strike our camp and head for home.
I have some choice
But when those creatures leap I find I am clean out of
  choice
And they draw blood so easily.
Dear family, as you awake,
And eye my campfire ashes nervously
I want to say how I am wretchedly aware
That others would protect and lead you properly.
They would be strong and confident and sure
They would be many things that I will never be
I only know they could not love you more.

Redundant Rituals and Flimsy Fashions

Fools may invent fashions that wise men will wear.

Thomas Fuller (*Gnomologia*, 1732)

Rituals, liturgies, credos, Sinai thunder: I know more or less the history of these; the rise, progress, decline and fall of these. Can thunder from all the thirty-two azimuths, repeated daily for centuries of years, make God's laws more godlike to me? Brother, no.

Thomas Carlyle (*Past and Present* III, 1843)

Redundant Rituals and Flimsy Fashions

Some months ago I spent a morning at a small independent evangelical church in Kent. I was speaking about the need for each individual to experience the kind of explosively joyful encounter that we read about in the parable of the prodigal son; that moment when the father throws his arms round his returning offspring and showers him with love, forgiveness and a host of practical gifts. Trying to follow Jesus without that experience, I was trying to say, is difficult, if not impossible, because love is the greatest motivator of all.

After I had finished, everyone broke off into small groups (where would the Church be without small groups?), to discuss three or four questions relating to the talk. As they 'discussed' I ambled around nervously, hoping that people were suitably stimulated and not sneaking covert glances at their watches every five minutes. Fortunately, all the groups seemed quite animated and had to be metaphorically prised apart so that we could enjoy our picnic lunch at one o'clock.

After lunch there was a brief feedback session (where would the Church be without brief feedback sessions?), and a short period of worship and prayer to round off the day.

'Good,' I said to myself, as the last 'amen' sounded. 'I can relax now. The talk went all right, the discussions went well, the people were nice – time to go home.'

It was as I lingered in conversation with a small group of elderly people at the back that I realized how miserably I had failed to convey my main point, at least as far as one person was concerned.

Her name was Beth, and she was one of those white-haired, attractive eighty-year-olds whose eyes are deeply crinkled from years of smiling. As I sat with Beth and two of her contemporaries someone mentioned outreach.

'I've always admired the old Sally Army,' said the venerable gentleman on Beth's right, 'the way they go into pubs and that with their papers. Maybe we should get to know people in the locals – then we could talk to 'em, couldn't we?'

'Not me,' said Beth, the crinkles disappearing as she sat up a little straighter in her chair, 'I would *never* do that!'

I looked at her for a moment.

'Suppose,' I said, 'that Jesus were to come through that back door now – today – and say "Beth, I want you to come down to the King's Head with me." Would you go?'

'I would not,' replied Beth, compressing her lips and folding her hands together decisively in her lap.

'But, Beth,' I persisted, 'we're talking about Jesus, the son of God, asking you personally if you would go with him. Would you not go?'

'I have never set foot in a public house in my life,' said the old lady adamantly, 'and I'm not about to start now.'

'But if Jesus himself asked – '

'It's a good witness,' interrupted Beth. 'Alcohol has never passed my lips and it never will.'

'Okay,' I said, warming to my theme, 'he doesn't want you to actually drink anything intoxicating, he just wants you with him in the King's Head, and – '

Beth shook her head firmly: 'No!'

'Jesus, God himself, the creator of everything, the reason

why we're all here today – he comes in and he says, "Beth, I really need you to come to the pub with me today, so *please*, please make an exception, just for me." Would you go with him?'

A tiny crack of uncertainty was undermining Beth's wall of principle. Her brows creased and her fingers twisted together as she mentally surveyed this rather unlikely scenario.

'I suppose,' she said at last, 'if he *really* did have a *really, really* good reason for asking, I *might* go.'

Afterwards, as I travelled home, I thought about Beth and the way in which her principles seemed to be a more powerful motivating force than the relationship she had with Jesus. I realized that my own sticking points were often more personal than spiritual. Was I so aware of the love of God that I would follow him wherever he went? Or would I, like the rich young man in the Bible, go away sorrowing because there was some principle or issue or sin or religious habit concerning which I simply would not budge?

The alarming truth is that these 'blocks' may well turn out to be respectable, laudable, even spiritual convictions or practices that have been elevated to the position of false gods.

Man-made fashions, fads and patterns can cause a lot of trouble as they work their way through the life of the Church. Here are quite a few examples in this last consignment of 'cabbages'.

Cabbages

I don't suppose God really minds what kind of spiritual activity we indulge in as long as we are expressing ourselves from the heart. The problem is that even the most impressively devout-sounding prayer, praise or worship might easily be nothing much more than a religious pattern.

Take prayer, for instance.

Two or three times a year I speak at dinners organized by a very energetic and effective body whose members are committed to outreach all over the world. I always enjoy these occasions, but I have noticed that a certain style of prayer seems to be mandatory for organizers and speaker before the evening gets going.

We stand in a tight circle with our arms round each other, like a small, introspective rugby scrum, bouncing on our heels (why?), shouting aggressive prayers towards the bottom of the well that is formed by our bodies. Eventually, someone will say something that sounds very much like: 'One hundred and eighty!'

Then we get on with the meal.

There's nothing wrong with this kind of prayer – who am I to criticize, anyway? It's just that habit can breed hollowness.

I couldn't help wondering what would happen if one of these violent-prayer merchants took over a greengrocer's shop, and, at the same time, happened to have no outlet for his religious fervour.

It might be a bit like this.

CABBAGES

Scene: *A Greengrocer's, Shopkeeper, Customer and a pile of cabbages.*

SHOPKEEPER: Good morning, madam. How may I help you?

CUSTOMER: I'd like a nice cabbage, please.

SHOPKEEPER: A nice cabbage?

CUSTOMER: Yes, please (*indicating*). That one will do nicely, thank you.

SHOPKEEPER: Just one moment, sister. That one will *not* do nicely.

CUSTOMER: It won't? Well, how about – ?

SHOPKEEPER: I think we should seek the will of God here. Do you witness to that, sister?

CUSTOMER: Well, I just want a cabbage really. I'm not sure –

SHOPKEEPER: Let's take it to the Lord. Let's just take it to him. (*Starts to pray*) Lord, we know that you chose a cabbage for our sister here before the world began, and we pray for your guidance now. We know that the world sees the outside of these cabbages, but, Lord, you see the inside. You see the heart. We pray that our sister's cabbage will have a heart for you, Lord.

We *claim* this cabbage! We *seal* this cabbage! Take dominion over your greens, Lord!

Lord, we ask that, like these fruits of thy bounty, we shall happily be sliced, boiled, drained

119

and consumed for you, Lord. Bless your chosen cabbage to our sister, Lord, and our sister to her rightful cabbage. Whether it be a companion to the sausage, Lord. Or, Lord, a neighbour to the fish-finger. Or peradventure Lord, an accessory to the veal cutlet: they and we are but coleslaw in your hands, and we just ask now that we shall make a decision according to your will.

Lord, we know that in your eyes there is no such thing as a Methodist cabbage, or a Pentecostal sprout, or a Strict and Particular turnip, or a Quaker carrot, or a United Reformed aubergine, or a Salvation Army swede, or a Baptist leek, or an Anglican potato. Lord, we're all just vegetables in your sight. And now we pray for your guidance on our sister's behalf.

And we say to the caterpillars of doubt and the slugs of uncertainty – we say 'Go! Right now! We rebuke you and we dismiss you and we cast you out from among these cabbages – right now!'

And now, Lord, we ask that your servant's appointed cabbage will just *rise up*! (*One cabbage springs into the air and is caught by the shopkeeper who drops it casually into a bag and hands it to the customer*) That'll be seventy-five pence, please.

CUSTOMER: Thank you! 'Morning! (*Exit*)

END

Doors

The language of the Bible and the Church (and the world, for that matter) is full of richness. Why, then, do so many choose to live in poverty? Are we frightened of language? Do we fear a serious distribution problem when, after taking all we need, we are left with twelve gloriously, extravagantly superfluous baskets of delicious, assorted words?

Take metaphor, for instance. We've only got about two. Here's one of them that may well have passed its sell-by date.

DOORS

INTERVIEWER: Now, Mr Williams, you and your wife have a recent experience of seeking guidance. Tell us about it, will you?

WILLIAMS: Well, what happened was – we tried one door that we thought the Lord was opening for us, but when, as it were, we pushed it, we found that it was shut. So we tried another door and this time it did open, so we passed through, and on the other side there was another door, but this one was shut like the first door. And when we turned round and tried to go back through the previous door – that is, the second door – we discovered that it had shut behind us, so we were in fact trapped between the two doors, so we had to climb out, as it were, through the skylight, and we came down through another skylight and found ourselves in front of, err ... a fourth door. This door was slightly ajar so I pushed it, but it was on a very strong spring, and it swung back and hit me quite hard on the face. So I did rebuke the door – and all the other doors, actually – at that stage, and we did wonder whether doorways might create openings through which something demonic can come. So we decided then to seek the Lord's will by laying a fleece, but ... well, the Lord shut that door.

INTERVIEWER: Mr Williams, what exactly were you and your wife seeking guidance over?

WILLIAMS: Whether to have an open-plan house or not...

Allegory

I am a great admirer of C. S. Lewis's Narnia books. Quite apart from pure entertainment value, they open up all sorts of ideas and perspectives that are interesting to juggle with. Most children love them, whatever some sniffy people may say, and you don't need to know anything about Christianity to enjoy them.

What about modern so-called 'Christian Books' for children? There are some good ones, of course, but I find the punch-in-the-mouth metaphors employed in some publications quite repellent, and I don't know what the point of such shallow writing could possibly be.

I could ramble on in this vein for page after page, but I've already written on the subject in one or two other books, and you're probably asking yourself how I can criticize other people for being shallow when I don't mind being boring.

All right! I give in – here is my own 'Allegory'.

ALLEGORY

'Where on earth is Flossy-Anne?'

Pimply's voice floated into the drawing-room from the patio outside the open French windows. Sticky and Fangio looked up from the sea of home-made bread, fresh eggs, boiled ham, farmhouse butter, thick strawberry jam, rich plum cake and creamy cow's milk that Auntie Enid made them plough through every time they came home for the hols.

Sticky was a sturdy twelve-year-old with an open, frank expression under fair sticking-up hair. Auntie Enid had called him Sticky since he was a little boy, not just because of his hair, but also because of a certain moistness in his handshake.

'I haven't seen Flossy-Anne for ages,' muttered Fangio. 'Sisters are nothing but a nuisance, aren't they, Sticky?'

The two friends grinned at each other. Sticky loathed eleven-year-old Pimply just as much as Fangio detested ten-year-old Flossy-Anne. Fangio was a dark, moody boy capable of manly impulses, but only very infrequently.

'I think she's still up in Auntie Enid's wardrobe,' called Sticky through a mouthful of half-masticated farmhouse butter.

'Oh, no, she's not looking for secret worlds again, is she?' Pimply's voice conveyed a mixture of exasperation and fondness as she ducked into the room. Well over six feet tall, Pimply had been given her nickname by Auntie Enid to take attention away from her height, but as her complexion deteriorated so she had seemed to 'grow into her name', as Auntie Enid put it.

'Well, what if I was? We haven't had a decent allegory for ages.'

The high, lisping voice coming from the doorway that led into the hall announced that the fourth member of the party was present. Fangio's younger sister, Flossy-Anne, was a fluffy-haired little girl with bulging eyes and a permanent expression of surprise on her face. One of her arms was slightly longer than the other.

'So there you all are!' The voice was muffled.

All eyes swivelled upwards towards the skylight, as Auntie Enid's face appeared behind the glass. Swinging the window open she dropped a rope-end into the room and was soon lowering her bikini-clad figure to the floor.

'I want a word with you lot!' she said. 'I've been trying to relax on the roof, and all I can hear is crashing noises. What's going on?'

Flossy-Anne turned bright purple and tried unsuccessfully to hide a small axe behind her back. The other children grinned at each other. Flossy-Anne always seemed to select the wrong arm!

'I'm afraid that was me,' she said. 'I was knocking out the back of your wardrobe, looking for Narnia. It wasn't there,' she added, looking so half-witted that even Auntie Enid had to laugh.

'You children and your allegories,' she smiled. 'Can't we have just one school holiday when you do something a bit less symbolic?'

Auntie Enid looked at her four charges with a mixture of fondness and exasperation. They all grinned at each other. Sticky, Pimply, Fangio and Flossy-Anne had been spending their school hols with Auntie Enid for the last twenty-four years. None of them ever grew any older, and they had never yet been known to use a lavatory.

'Look at what happened yesterday,' said Auntie Enid, 'Sticky tried to get into the picture on his bedroom wall, didn't you, Sticky?'

Sticky grinned.

'And the day before that I had to call the fire brigade to rescue Fangio from the bottom of that old hollow oak tree at the bottom of the garden.'

Fangio looked at her with a mixture of fondness and exasperation.

'It's all very well for you, Auntie Enid,' he said, 'you're an adult Christian. Life is one long spiritual adventure for you. We kids have difficulty understanding that. We need to experience reality through synchronistic fantasy. Besides, after twenty-four years we're allegory junkies. We need our fix, and that's why we're all hunting for this summer's secret entrance. I'm going to have a look down the lavatory bowl tomorrow – after all, it's quite hygenic because we never use it.'

Auntie Enid sighed. 'Well, I don't know what to say. I've grinned, and I've looked at you with a mixture of fondness and exasperation. What more can I do?'

'Well, I think Auntie Enid's right,' said Pimply earnestly. 'Why can't we stay here and go to church and have real adventures with God like the grown-ups do?'

Although Fangio detested his sister he was very fond of her as well. He hated to see her make a fool of herself.

'Pimply,' he said kindly, 'it's got to be allegory because allegory sells where spiritual adventure won't. Think secular, think W. H. Smith, think Waterstone's, think Dillons. If nobody reads us we don't exist, right?'

'I'll check the cellar for secret doors tomorrow,' said Pimply.

They all grinned at each other.

Playing Games

Our writer now seems to have been resurrected. He's back on earth and getting a bit worried about his royalties – if there are any.

In every area of specifically Christian work the tension between commercial and spiritual considerations can produce all sorts of games that have to be played out appropriately before a resolution can be reached.

I do hope old Rodney gets what he really needs.

PLAYING GAMES

W = Writer
P = Publisher

W: Hello, Crystal, it's Rodney here – Rodney Fuller.

P: Rodney! Great! How *are* you? Great to hear your voice!

W: I'm fine, Crystal. I was just ringing to ask how the book's going.

P: The book! Well –

W: Yes, my children's allegory – *Slubglab's Splod.*

P: Ah, right! Well, Rodney, we feel tremendously encouraged!

W: You do? By the sales, you mean?

P: We regard your book as a very significant addition to our back-list.

W: Oh! But in terms of sales – I wondered – I mean – things are a bit tight. I wondered if there are going to be royalties coming up when –

P: Rodney, we're all of us – publishers and writers – part of the Lord's team in this, aren't we? That's my priority, anyway.

W: Mmm ... it's just that you don't seem to have put much into publicity, really.

P: You have to bear in mind that publishing is a commercial operation, Rodney. We can't afford to be airy-fairy, can we? Publicity is expensive.

W: Well, how many copies have actually been sold?

P: We're tremendously encouraged!

W: Yes, you said that before, but you still haven't told me the actual figures.

P: Okay, let me put it like this – the moment we hit the five thousand mark we'll be reprinting immediately – or sooner!

W: I've sold nearly five thousand then?

P: Well, no, but if we ever did hit the five thousand mark we'd –

W: Crystal, how many books have I sold?

P: What do we get from tiny acorns, Rodney?

W: Mighty oaks! How many books have I sold?

P: How many people did our Lord use as a basis for the world-wide Church?

W: Twelve! How many books – wait a minute! Are you saying that I've sold *twelve* copies? Twelve! You told me that this book was going to change the face of children's literature in the twentieth century! How's it going to do that if only twelve people have bought it?

P: Of course I didn't mean that, Rodney. We have had a little problem – err ... just after your book came out we found there was already a children's book on the market called *Slodglub's Slab*, which is not unlike *Slubglab's Splod*, so that did create a titchy-witchy problem. But, no, your sales are well up in the high, err ... well, err ... well, well, we're tremendously encouraged.

W: I'm fed up with this, Crystal! I might as well tell you – I've got myself an agent.

P: You've what? An agent? Rodney, this is terrible! This is – wait a minute. Is he a Christian?

W: Yes, he is.

P: Ah, that's all right then...

END

Trapeze

When I first started writing I was advised to 'study the market'. This is very good advice, especially for anyone who wants to write for a particular type of magazine or journal. I bought all the Christian magazines and newspapers and looked through them to see what sort of thing I should be producing.

As far as I could see, the most popular type of article was one in which someone who had just written a book lectured his or her readers, gently but firmly, on the subject of their failure to perform satisfactorily in some crucial area of their lives. The article would be accompanied by a box containing five, eight or even ten handy points to remind readers how it should be done. I tried to write such an article myself, but I didn't feel very comfortable about it.

It was only Andy Butcher's inventiveness and Mary Reid's courage that enabled something as unusual as the *Sacred Diary!* to appear, as it originally did, in column form in *Family Magazine*.

My advice to a new writer nowadays would be very similar to that which I received, except that I would add something. Once you have studied the market and thoroughly understood it – do something different. Do something that reflects what, where and who you are. Find out who created whatever boundaries you come across and, if it wasn't God, look at them very carefully indeed.

I very much enjoyed writing the piece that follows, but I do hope the style and content that I am caricaturing will go the way of the dinosaurs before too long. If you want an example of Chrisitan literature with a real edge – try the Bible.

TRAPEZE

Trembling with fear, the elderly lady gripped the trapeze bar so tightly that her knuckles whitened under the pressure. Glancing down at the sawdust floor a hundred feet below the tiny platform on which she balanced, she silently asked herself yet again, why, at the age of eighty-three, she was about to leap into space, supported only by the slender length of wood that her arthritic hands were clutching with such nervous intensity. Moistening dry lips with the tip of her tongue she tried hard to remember the advice that Dave and Sheena had given her.

'Don't look down – concentrate on what's happening up here. Remember that God created gravity as well as everything else ...'

Suddenly it was time to go. Gently but firmly, Dave's hands pressed into the small of her back until she toppled over the edge of the platform and found herself swinging out and across the open space beneath the canvas ceiling of the huge tent. There was a moment's exhilaration followed by a stab of fear as she felt the bar sliding slowly but inexorably from her grasp. Dimly she was aware of Sheena's encouraging smile as the opposite trapeze swung past, and then she was falling down and down until, with a bone-shuddering jar, her body hit the safety-net, bounced two or three times, then came to rest like a pound of sausages in a string-bag. A few bruises, a minor fracture here and there perhaps, but, as the octogenarian acrobat was lifted carefully from the net, there was a smile on her face. A faint cry of 'Hallelujah!' from the platform high above indicated Dave's awareness that he and Sheena had yet another satisfied 'customer'!

It is ten years since Dave Bolden, now a slim and well-preserved man in his early forties, first realized that God was telling him, in no uncertain terms, that acrobatics on the high trapeze are for the whole Church, not just for a specially selected few.

'I fought against it for a while,' says Dave, his handsome face breaking into a grin as he remembers, 'but after a couple of falls from a hundred feet without a safety net I began to think very seriously about the direction I was going in. The Lord has such a sense of humour!' he chuckles.

What about scriptural support for these revelations?

'Let's face it,' avers Dave wryly, 'you can prove or disprove just about anything you like if you don't mind twisting Bible verses to make them fit the truth as you want to see it. I have to say, though, that my own reading of Acts in particular suggests that, possibly Peter, and certainly Paul the apostle, were very fine performers on the flying trapeze in their own right. In fact, it seems clear to me that aerial acrobatics was a normal and acceptable part of day-to-day life in the early Church. It's fallen into disuse in this age and we just want to do something about it.'

Did Dave encounter any special problems in setting up his ministry?

An awe-struck expression appears on Dave's well-chiselled features. 'It was a real miracle, especially when it came to getting a big top.' He shakes his head in disbelief. 'I was literally led step by step. I bought a magazine called *Big Tops for Sale* – quite by chance, you understand – and I was flicking idly through it one day, when an advert seemed to leap off the page, and hit me between the eyes. It said "Big Top for sale" and there was a telephone number.'

Dave's attractive and expertly made-up wife, Sheena, takes up the story, her green eyes shining with excitement.

'I dialled the number and when I spoke to the man at the other end I could hardly believe my ears. He had a big top for sale! The amount of money he wanted was almost exactly the amount of money that we had to spend.'

Dave picks up the thread.

'We weren't quite sure what to do then, so we rang around our Christian friends for advice.' Tears well up in Dave's eyes as he continues. 'It was amazing! They *all* said the same thing. Why not suggest to the man that we give him the amount of money he wants and he gives us his big top in exchange? When we rang him back and put this to him he agreed on the spot, and that seemed like a sort of final confirmation. We were so excited that Sheena leaped up on to my shoulders and did a double backward somersault with pike and triple twist into my paternal grandfather who was staying at the time.'

Sheena giggles, showing two rows of perfectly formed teeth.

'I did get a little excited,' she confesses with a mischievous twinkle, 'but grandpops understood – once he regained consciousness.'

They laugh and look into each other's eyes. This couple are still very much in love.

Over the course of the last decade many folk have 'swung for God' as Dave pursues his deeply held conviction that the Lord would have all his people involved in high trapeze work. Have some sections of the Church been less ready to respond than others?

Dave nods seriously. 'The elderly infirm have been very sluggish in their response, so too have partially-sighted and blind folk. They are particularly reluctant to step off the platform once we get them up there.' His normally cheerful face clouds over suddenly. 'I guess it's a matter of trust. The world says it makes no sense to step into space a hundred feet above the ground when you're blind and have no experience of trapeze work, but we are not of the world and ought to be different really.'

Are there dangers?

The old smile returns to Dave's face. He catches Sheena's eye and they both laugh. They've been asked this question many times in the past.

'Let me put it like this,' he explains. 'It's far less dangerous than strolling across the M25 with a blindfold on when the traffic is moving at maximum speed. Why do anything as risky as that when you could be here doing something really worthwhile?'

The question seems unanswerable and, in any case, there is no time for a reply. In the distance two men can be seen stretchering in the next candidate for high-flying obedience. With a flashing smile from Sheena, and a friendly wave from Dave, the trim couple are gone. Christians are often told that it's a good thing to keep their 'feet on the ground'. People who know Dave and Sheena Bolden are not quite so sure!

DAVE BOLDEN'S FIVE HELPFUL HINTS

1) **DO** contact your nearest circus and ask how accessible they are prepared to be to church members. Christians have a God-given right to the use of trapeze equipment.

2) **DON'T** be afraid to insure your life before 'taking the plunge'. Christians are not called upon to abandon commonsense just because they're doing what God has told them to do!

3) **DO** speak to your vicar, elder, or church leader about wanting to perform acrobatics a hundred feet above the ground. He will certainly have some helpful things to say.

4) **DON'T** be put off by 'horror stories' spread by others. People who talk about death and serious injury are very rarely the ones who have actually suffered such things.

5) **DO** remember that non-believing circus employees will be watching as you ascend to that little platform. If you're up there with a long face, and 'I FEEL TENSE' written all over you, what are they going to make of the Christian faith? Enjoy yourself – and let it show!

Starting a Meeting

I have included the following piece at the last moment because it was inspired by a sermon that I heard just the other day. If you can imagine Basil Fawlty, converted but not changed, making his convoluted way through the business of starting a meeting in a very 'unadorned' church, then you will easily picture the chap who is delivering this 'message'.

I would have included the rest of his talk, but a book can only be so long, and I fear your head would spin off and go into orbit. It might anyway.

STARTING A MEETING

Can I start by suggesting that if I come back *now* to something I shall have said earlier, it will save a great deal of time in a minute? Is that clear?

I'm going to begin by telling a humorous story. The purpose of this is to relax you, the congregation, so that you will be more receptive to the serious points that I shall subsequently make. So, if you are taking notes I would suggest that you refrain from recording any of the first section because it will *be* the humorous story. Do, however, feel free to record the humorous story if you would like to pass it on to somebody else after the service, though naturally there will be no point in passing on the humorous story to anyone who is present now because, of course, they will have already heard it, unless, that is, they have to leave in the middle of the humorous story, before its climactic peak has been reached.

After the humorous story is concluded, and the laughter thus engendered has died away, I shall speak under three headings, each beginning with a 'P': Plague, Punishment and Pestilence – three areas which, I believe, beautifully illustrate the love of God.

But first, as promised, the relaxing humorous story. Those of you who are feeling tense this morning will, in a minute or so, be relaxed enough to hear scriptural judgement pronounced upon those of us for whom it is intended.

This humorous story is one which, in its original form, is quite unsuitable for the elect. I have therefore adapted the content so that it is no less humorous, but considerably more edifying.

It concerns a male person who questions another male person in the following fashion.

'Who was that lady I saw you with last night?'

The other male person replies in tones of righteous, but quite justifiable, indignation, with these words.

'The lady in question happens to be my marital partner, and has been so for some three decades.'

I shall wait a few moments now while the laughter provoked by the humorous story runs its course. Settle down please.

Well, that is the end of the fun section and now I feel sure that most of us are more than ready for our first 'P' of the morning.

Plague! And how we do need it in the Church today ...

Images of God

The worship of false images is not a sin that tends to be discussed very much in the twenty-first-century Church. When it *is* mentioned it's usually equated with excessive attachment to possessions, such as cars or houses. After all, you don't see too many golden calves or images of Baal in your average British sitting-room.

There is, however, another, and more subtly destructive way in which this commandment continues to be disobeyed – by Christians.

We all do it to a lesser or greater extent. Because of individual upbringing, life experiences and inherited patterns of response, we tend to invest our personal images of God with attributes that have more to do with us than with God as he actually is.

Often, and perhaps more commonly, people have difficulty in separating the concept of God as father, from memories of their own unsatisfactory parent. Earthly fathers can be cruel or over-indulgent or emotionally chaotic. The child in us clings unconsciously to these negative recollections, unable to allow the idea of God as a perfect father to sink successfully from head to heart.

Within any one congregation a strange and varied selection of God-images will be prayed to and worshipped each Sunday.

I have recorded elsewhere how a friend of mine on hearing Bishop Peter Ball talk about his faith, said, 'He knows a different God to the one I do – his God's nice!'

There are many distorted views of the divine personality. Here are three of the most common ones.

IMAGES OF GOD

1) **God as Bank Manager**
   Ah, Mr Brown, do please sit down,
   Now what are we to do?
   For, once, you banked with us, but now,
   We seem to bank with you.
   Your sin account is overdrawn,
   With lust and sloth and pride,
   And, dear, dear, dear, there's little here,
   Upon the credit side.
   Against the veritable sea,
   Of evil you have done,
   There's one small act of kindness,
   Back in nineteen-sixty-one.
   In fact your banking record,
   From the moment you were born,
   Is such that we may well decide,
   Your Access is withdrawn.

2) **God as a Senile Old Man**
   Hello! Yes, this is God – speak up!
   Hello! What's that you say?
   Well, if you say you did, you did,
   I didn't hear you pray.
   You say you asked me several times?
   Well, nowadays I find,

That even quite important things
Just seem to slip my mind.
Oh, yes, that is a problem,
But there's little I can do,
My angels are quite elderly,
They've all got fowlpest too.
I wouldn't bother being good,
You'll only end up bored,
It's not exactly heaven,
In a geriatric ward.

3) **God as a Hippy**
Nothing's wrong and nothing's right,
And nothing's in between,
All this 'Heh, you broke the rules',
Has never been my scene.
People go for different things.
Like Mecca and Nirvana,
Some find me in worry beads,
Or hash, or a banana.
Don't let people steer you wrong,
It's cool to sin and doubt,
Whatever gives you groovy vibes,
Just let it all hang out.
Heaven's what you make it, man,
Freedom gives you power,
Love and peace and jelly-beans,
No hassle – have a flower.

Connections to Paradise

People often ask me where writers get their ideas from. The answer, of course, is – British Rail. No, I'm only joking, although, when you travel by train as much as I do, you do hear some wonderful things. Take the other day, for instance. I was sitting on a train, in a fairly crowded compartment, when the guard's voice came over the loudspeaker system. It began in that flatly repetitive tone beloved of guards everywhere, but it quite quickly turned into a strangled bleat.

'Like to advise customers that the next station stop will be Darnley Halt. (*Pause*) Darnley Halt has a very short platform. (*Longer pause*) Customers wishing to alight at Darnley Halt should move to the front of the train. The front of the train (*Worried pause*) is situated (*Very worried pause*) at the end (*Pause indicative of realization that there is no way out of sentence with honour*) farthest (*Pause of utter panic*) from (*Pause as guard plays wildly with alternative endings to his sentence, such as: ' ... the Platonic Ideal', or 'Patagonia'*) the back ...' (*Miserable silence as guard covers head with arms and vows to stay locked in little guard compartment for rest of journey*)

No, it isn't always British Rail, but it's certainly true that most of my ideas spring from relatively ordinary day-to-day incidents.

'Yes,' says the questioner when I explain this, 'but nothing ever happens to me – nothing worth recording in detail, anyway.'

I don't think this is true. Lots of different things happen to all of us; the difference, perhaps, is that the writer makes a conscious mental (or written) note of his or her experiences and, even more importantly, goes on to forge or discover the kind of connections that add depth and significance to quite ordinary observations.

Let me give you an example.

CONNECTIONS TO PARADISE

One morning I was travelling by train from Poleg-ate, in Sussex, down to Southampton for a day of promotion in connection with my latest book. I knew I had to change at Brighton, but I wasn't quite sure whether the journey was straight through after that. I went into the travel-centre on Brighton station to check.

Travel-centres are strange places. They seem to be staffed by people who go off sick in packs of four. They always leave behind a nice but nervy person who will burst into tears if too much pressure is put on them. In addition, the queue in front of you invariably consists of a ninety-year-old Ukranian who speaks no English, weeps passionately but inexplicably at regular intervals, and needs to get to Clitheroe via Taunton on a sleeper in six weeks' time, and a very, very lonely person who always comes down there on that day, at that time, to while away an hour or so with the nice, nervy person who doesn't mind because it never involves any nasty, awkward questions about train times.

Thank goodness Brighton travel-centre is nothing like that. I had no trouble at all.

'Change at Hove, sir,' trilled the young girl behind the counter, 'you'll pick up a Southampton train there.'

'Thank you!' I called over my shoulder as I went back out to the station concourse.

On my way to the appropriate platform I glanced up at the electronic information board, just hoping for a little comfortable confirmation. No such luck!

'*Passengers for Southampton should change at Worthing*', announced the board in large white letters.

Somewhat dismayed, I stopped at the ticket barrier and spoke to the bored young man who was slumped on a stool inside his little shelter.

'Tell me,' I said, 'if you were me, where would you change for Southampton on this train?'

'Portsmouth,' he replied with gloomy certainty.

'Portsmouth?' I repeated. 'Are you sure?'

'Change at Portsmouth for Southampton,' he said, in that wearily sarcastic manner that people reserve for those who haven't understood the first time.

Muttering thanks I hurried along the platform to board my train, and was just about to get on when I surrendered to a wild impulse to ask just once more for this surprisingly elusive piece of information. An elderly, white-haired, rather avuncular looking British Rail employee was pushing a trolley past me. This was a man to be trusted – a man who would know!

'Excuse me,' I called.

The man stopped his trolley and beamed at me with fatherly kindness. 'Ow can I 'elp you, sir?' he said.

I explained that I had been offered three quite different pieces of advice and wasn't sure which one to follow. He chuckled tolerantly.

'Bless 'em, sir, they don't know nothin', these young things. If you take this train you wanna change at Havant for Southampton, sir. You'll pick one up there all right.'

'Oh well,' I said to myself as I settled down in the corner of a carriage at last, 'at least I know now – change at Havant ...'

A few minutes later the ticket inspector arrived. He was a youngish man with a heavy Indian accent.

'Change at Havant for Southampton, don't I?' I enquired lightly, certain that he would agree.

'You need to go upstairs, sir,' he replied, 'upstairs for Southampton.'

I stared at him for a moment, my senses reeling. Upstairs? Upstairs for Southampton? Had I, without realizing it, boarded some kind of new double-decker train, the top half of which went to Southampton, while the bottom half didn't? How could that be ...?

'Upstairs?' I repeated faintly, 'I don't ...'

'Upstairs at Portsmouth station,' continued my informant, 'upstairs to the upper platform for the train to Southampton, sir. That is what you must do.'

And that piece of advice was, I'm pleased to say, absolutely correct.

That is what happened, and it is completely true.

Connections? Well, it occurred to me afterwards that my succession of advisers, all employed by the same company, and all offering diverse views on the same subject, were rather like the Christian denominations, each with its own clear idea about how people should get to the place where they are going, and each adamant that their way is the only one worth considering.

Where *do* we change for Paradise?

Precious

For years I tried to exercise ministries that I had not got. It didn't work.

I did *not* have a ministry of reconciliation. I had a ministry of making things worse, and ending up with everyone disliking me as well as each other.

I did *not* have a ministry of wisdom and special insight. I had a ministry of getting things wrong and upsetting people.

I did *not* have a ministry of prayer. I had a ministry of promising people I would pray for them, and then forgetting to do it, and getting very embarrassed when they thanked me and said that they knew my prayers had helped, and feeling guilty because I couldn't quite bring myself to tell them the truth.

I did *not* have a ministry of evangelism. I had a ministry of putting forward arguments so hopelessly ill-prepared and half-baked that I became progressively less convinced myself as I went on speaking, and ended up in a state of miserable agnosticism.

I did *not* have a ministry of prophetic absailing, although it broke my heart to have finally to face that realization.

Perhaps there are signs of a genuine ministry developing nowadays, but I'm certainly not going to put a name to what I think it might be.

Here's a ludicrously exaggerated version of what goes wrong when a 'ministry of encouragement' is exercised so liberally that the encouragement becomes devalued to the point of being rather meaningless.

PRECIOUS

Leader, Stanley, George (a newcomer), Veronica and
Penelope are sitting in a semi-circle. They all have
open Bibles on their laps.

LEADER: Right, now, we've read the passage of Scripture that tells us the story of Zacchaeus, and I'm
going to ask that we might share our insights as we
feel led so to do.
(*Pause*)

STANLEY: Well, I was thinking ...

LEADER: Yes, Stanley, go ahead.

GEORGE: Yeah, go fer it, Stan!

STANLEY: Well, I was thinking that Zacchaeus was up
a tree, and a tree's got leaves, right?

LEADER: Yes?

STANLEY: Yes, and God *leaves* us to deal with certain
things on our own. He *leaves* us, doesn't he?

LEADER: Well, isn't that interesting? *Isn't* that interesting? Do you know – I never made that connection before. Leaves on the tree, and he *leaves* us.
Isn't that interesting? (*Pause*) Any other insights to
share?

VERONICA: I noticed that Zacchaeus begins with the
last letter of the alphabet, and, when you think of
it, the last thing God wants us to do is disobey him.
It's the last thing he wants us to do, and Zacchaeus
begins with the *last* letter of the alphabet.

LEADER: Isn't that special? That's *very* special. The last
thing God wants is disobedience, and Zacchaeus
begins with ... that's very special – *very* special.

Veronica has given us something very special, hasn't she, everybody?

(*All nod except George, who shakes his head in puzzlement*)

PENELOPE: May I share?

LEADER: Please do, Penelope. Mmmm!

PENELOPE: I feel that this passage is really about serving. Zacchaeus was asked to serve – not just serve the food, but to serve the Lord. We should all serve. He's called us to serve, and when we do serve we in our turn will be served. Not just serving because we're told to serve, but serving with joy because we want to serve the one who served us.

LEADER: Isn't that precious? What a precious thing to share. We're called to serve – we're all called to serve each other. What a new and precious thought. Bless you, Penelope, for that very precious gift to us. (*Pause*) George, you're new here, but have you any err...

GEORGE: Well, I'm not sure I've got the 'ang of this, but I was thinkin' that once old Zack was –

LEADER: Zacchaeus.

GEORGE: Once old Zacchaeus was – like – back on the ground ...

LEADER: Yes?

GEORGE: Well, everyone must've realized 'e was a scone short of a cream tea, mustn't they?

LEADER: A scone short of ...? Do you mean that he was mentally deranged?

GEORGE: Yeah, that's right, yeah.

LEADER: And why must everyone have realized that?

GEORGE: Well, s'obvious, innit? Because ... (*Pause*) 'e

was out of 'is tree! Out of 'is tree – gettit? 'E was out of 'is tree!

(*Laughs raucously*)

LEADER: (*When George has finished laughing*) Well, isn't that silly. That's *very* silly. That was a silly thing to share, wasn't it, everybody?

GEORGE: Why? 'Ow come 'is was interestin', an' 'ers was special, an 'ers was precious, but mine's silly? Anyway, Precious laughed, didn't you Precious? Old Special looked a bit upset, but Precious was well away, weren't you, Precious? Couldn't 'elp it, could yer?

PENELOPE: (*No longer laughing*) If you call me Precious one more time I shall break my chair over your head!

GEORGE: Well, that's special, innit? That's interestin'. That's a very precious gift to me, innit? Breakin' a chair over me 'ead! (*To Penelope*) Thank you for offering to share your chair with me. What d'yer make of that, chief? I bet old Zacchaeus wouldn't 'ave done that once 'e got Jesus 'ome an' sat down at the table – crept up behind 'im an' broken a chair over 'is 'ead. I bet –

STANLEY: May I share an urge?

(*Pause*)

GEORGE: (*Warily*) That's interestin', innit?

STANLEY: I'd like to suggest that we forgive our brother George fully and freely, just as Zacchaeus was forgiven for all his past offences.

LEADER: Well, isn't that lovely. *Isn't* that lovely! Isn't that a lovely unselfish thought, everybody?

GEORGE: Yeah, that's lovely all right. Only reason I'm 'ere is 'cos old Stan 'adn't got a lift tonight, an' 'e knows 'e won't get 'ome unless 'e does a grease-job on yours truly. That's a lovely unselfish thought, Stan, old mate. That's –

LEADER: Just a minute. Did you really give Stanley a lift here tonight, George? Did you do that for him?

GEORGE: Well ... yeah, I did.

LEADER: Well, isn't that ... That's really ... (*Searches for appropriate word*)

PENELOPE: Surprising?

LEADER: Now, now, Precious – I mean – Penelope, there is something very beautiful about George bringing Stanley here in his car without any thought of personal cost. Isn't that beautiful, everybody?

STANLEY: He charged me the same as a taxi would have done – Sunday rate. That's double.

LEADER: Oh! Well, that's not quite so beautiful, is it?

GEORGE: Ah, well I *'ad* to charge 'im, see?

LEADER: You had to?

GEORGE: Yeah! I needed the money for the same reason that old Zacchaeus 'ad to climb the tree.

LEADER: And that reason was ...?

GEORGE: Well, like old Zacchaeus...

LEADER: Yes?

GEORGE: I was a bit short. Gettit? A bit short! (*Laughs*)

LEADER: Let's close by joining together in a physical attack on George. Won't that be lovely?

STANLEY: That's a very interesting prospect.

VERONICA: Very special.

PENELOPE: Precious!

(*They converge on him*)

END

Gig-Along-a-God

Our writer has now had a stroke of really bad luck. The poor fellow has been renamed Cedric Spamrumbler (as if he hadn't got enough problems already). He is about to come face to face with the 'famous Christian' machine, that strange mechanism that takes very ordinary people and turns them into *well-known* very ordinary people.

The significant point, of course, is that dear old Cedric is very anxious to meet his hypothetical public halfway. Once he's established he'll be free to say that fame and popularity were never motivating forces in his 'ministry'.

Oh, Cedric!

GIG-ALONG-A-GOD

W = Writer
A = Agent

W: Good morning – err ... is this the agency?
A: Yes, indeed, sir, we are the Gig-Along-a-God Christian Performance Agency: Charismatics for Conferences, Prophets for Parties, Evangelicals for Events, Bible-scholars for Beanos, Mystics for Mainstage, Marquees and Marriages, Healers for Hoe-downs, Parsons for Picnics and Theologians

for Theatricals; Bless-O-Grams a speciality; all prices include VAT and will be tithed at source. Is your social engagement heading for disaster? My name is Grace. How may I serve you?

W: Well, err ... I want to be a cult.

A: You want to be ...?

W: I want to be on the fringe at Green Harvest and Springbelt. I want to be famous! I want to be recognized! I want some respect! I want to be a star!! (*Pause*) ... for the Lord ...

A: Our brochure does guarantee humility in *all* performers, Mister err ...

W: Spamrumbler – Cedric Spamrumbler

A: Well, that would certainly keep *me* humble. So, Mister Spamrumbler – what is your normal occupation?

W: Well, I'm a Christian writer – it's a very lonely job y'know. I thought maybe a bit of public exposure might make life a bit brighter and push the sales a bit and – (*Suddenly crazed*) I wanna sign autograph books! I want to be endearingly self-effacing when I'm interviewed in front of hundreds of people! I want –

A: Mister Spamrumbler, what was the title of your last book?

W: It was called *An Exegetical Analysis of Philosophical Infrastructures in Post-Alluvial Didacticism* – Volume nine.

A: Hmmm ... not the sort of thing you can turn into a musical, is it? Are there any funny bits in it?

W: There are some references to mythical incongruity in the context of evolutionary antitheses that certainly make me chuckle.

A: Mmm, yes, what a hoot ... I'm not sure we're quite getting there yet, Mister Spamrumbler. What about something juicy in the past that you've had a wonderful deliverance from? That always goes down very well. Ever been on drugs? Drink? Contact with the occult? Been in prison? Ever been involved with some big scandal in the papers – 'Playboy Peer Slams Neo-nazi Darby and Joan Club' – that sort of thing?

W: The only thing I can remember ... (*Glances guiltily round*) well – last year I slightly over-filled my salad bowl during a visit to my local Pizza Land restaurant. I don't know why I did it. I – I just lost my head!

A: Mmm, yes, I think we can do something with that. 'Greed Leads Top Christian Academic to Defraud Huge Food Chain'. I'll get that in the Christian press for the month after next. Tomorrow morning I'll get on to a contact at the publisher's and have a contract drawn up for – let's say – a 40,000-word paperback, thousand pound advance. Title – let's see; something like: 'From Gluttony to God – one man's journey from the gutter of slavering, greed and lust to the peace of personal renewal'. Be out by next spring – and we should have you doing seminars on Dieting, Gluttony, Anorexia, Cookery, Significance of Bread in the New Testament, and Occult Influence on the Pizza – by, well, by autumn at the earliest. How does that sound, Mister Spamrumbler?

W: Well, it sounds fine! What about money? How much will I have to pay you?

A: It's customary to pay a percentage to the agent, Mister Spamrumbler.

W: I see. Well, do you think we ought to pray about what the percentage should be?

A: Err … yes, all right. Let's err … pray that we will be told the appropriate figure.

(*They both pray*)

W: Ten per cent!

A: (*Almost simultaneously*) Fifteen per cent! Mmm, let's give it a few more seconds…

(*They pray*)

W & A: (*Simultaneously*) Twelve and a half per cent!

(*They stand and shake hands*)

END

Anglican Rap

When I told my children I was contemplating the writing of a 'Rap' they were far from impressed. I think they had visions of me performing some sonorous piece of badly scanning verse whose aim was to show the youth of today that the Church is relevant to their culture. They needn't have worried. I have a deep and abiding dislike of arranged marriages between two concepts that repel each other on sight.

We have enough things in the Christian faith that are authentically and uniquely ours, without having to caper foolishly to the world's tune. Don't misunderstand me – I'm all for minimum silliness and proper cultural integration. It's the Saatchi and Saatchi approach that puts me off. Why construct a false presentation of something that's true anyway? Much better, surely, to strip away the man-made nonsense that has obscured the truth, a truth that always *was* relevant. I would rather go to a properly conducted bar, selling all the normal alcoholic drinks, and run by Christians, than crouch over my vimto in a so-called 'Christian bar'. But, of course, I may be quite wrong in taking that view, and how fortunate I am that those of you who *do* disagree with me will freely forgive me for my error.

The 'Anglican Rap' is a light-hearted look at what might result from my own church's attempt to preserve itself in its most turgid form by using a 'modern' device.

ANGLICAN RAP

Let's kneel, let's stand,
Let's be terribly bland,
Let's sing quite loud with a dignified clap,
Let's process around the church in a victory lap.
Check us on the old denominational map,
From the Isle of Wight to the Watford Gap,
Everybody's doing it – the Anglican rap.
Come along and boogie to the Anglican beat,
Just grab your hermeneutics and exegete!

Take a cruise to the pews, have a snooze, read the news,
Don't go looking for disaster with a Pentecostal pastor,
There'll be tongues and revelations with bizarre
    interpretations.
Don't smile when life's vile in the house-church style,
Or linger with the lost under old Rob Frost.
Do you fancy looking barmy with the silly Sally Army?
Don't meet above the baker's with the Shakers and the
    Quakers,
Or shiver in the water like the Baptists say you oughter,
We don't baptize in the bottom of a tank,
Our font is Norman, and our vicar is Frank.
We're well aware of modern theological trends,
But Frank and Norman are still good friends.
We're modern and we're modish, have you seen our
    groovy cassocks?
And we're open to the option of inflated rubber
    hassocks.
Be a real cool cat, be an Anglican dude,
Every now and then we're *almost* rude.

Let's kneel, let's stand,
Let's be terribly bland.
Let's sing quite loud with a dignified clap,
Let's process around the church in a victory lap.
Check us on the old denominational map,
From the Isle of Wight to the Watford Gap,
Everybody's doing it – the Anglican rap.
Come along and boogie to the Anglican beat,
Just grab your hermeneutics and exegete.

Don't falter at the altar, have a rave in the nave,
Have a smile in the aisle, have a lapse in the apse,
Have a thriller by the pillar, eat an apple in the chapel,
Have some oysters in the cloisters, read some Auden to
      the warden,
Climb the font if you want, feel the power up the tower,
Light a torch in the porch, start a fire in the choir,
Raise your arms in the psalms, mind the gorgon at the
      organ,
Swap your knickers for the vicar's, check you're zipped
      in the crypt.
Some of us speak through tightly clenched teeth,
And lots of us look like Edward Heath. (And that's just
      the ladies)
Anglicans hurry to the old God-shack,
To be first in the queue for the seats at the back.
We're a very broad church, we're home from home,
You can chat up the vicar, or flirt with Rome.
The leader of our gang is big and scary,
He's no spring-chicken, but his name is Carey.

Let's kneel, let's stand,
Let's be terribly bland,
Let's sing quite loud with a dignified clap,

Let's process around the church in a victory lap.
Check us on the old denominational map,
From the Isle of Wight to the Watford Gap,
Everybody's doing it – the Anglican rap.
Come along and boogie to the Anglican beat,
Just grab your hermeneutics and exegete!

Dear Craig

A friend of mine who happens to be gay and a Christian went through hell in his early attempts to find counselling and constructive assistance from various sections of the Church. Elementary formulae and simplistic ideas were not just unhelpful – they were sometimes terrifying. Now, thank God, he has found people and places that offer hope, because they are dealing with *him*, rather than one aspect of what he is.

That is the Jesus way.

Perhaps we should think before we produce clichéd responses to very deep problems. The following letter is extremely silly but ...

DEAR CRAIG

Dear Craig,

First of all, let me say how much I appreciate the fact that you have trusted me with such a delicate and personal problem. I only hope I can help a little!

Craig, I'm going to say something to you now that may surprise you. I very much doubt that you really are the only person in your church who owns a trombone. Recent and quite reliable research shows that at least one in twenty-five of all British males is in possession of a brass instrument of some kind, and yours is a large congregation. I am quite sure you are not alone.

And now for a little personal testimony. This is a private letter, so you will understand that what follows is not for sharing, A few years ago, Craig, I inherited the possessions of an elderly uncle whom I had known only slightly. When I arrived at Uncle Brendon's house to look through the items that were now mine, I discovered that my uncle had himself been the covert owner of a brass instrument. For some reasons that I do not understand I was both repulsed and fascinated by the object. Throwing all moral considerations to the wind I raised the instrument to my lips (I will not mince words with you, Craig) and blew one indulgent blast that shattered the silence of my deceased uncle's bedroom.

Guilt encased me like a diving-suit, Craig.

Later that day I arrived home, sat my wife quietly down in the kitchen, and, taking both her hands in mine, told her as gently as I could that I now had a malignant tuba.

Clarissa and I have worked through that problem as man and wife, and I think I can honestly say that it is under control. I shall always have my tuba, but it has not left the closet since that day.

I inherited my wind instrument, Craig, and some people claim that they cannot be acquired in any other way. You do not say in your letter anything about the origin of your brass instrument, but I am convinced in my own mind that inheritance is not the only means by which younger *and* older folk become involved in such pursuits. (I once counselled a tone-deaf pensioner who had embezzled a tenor saxophone.)

Craig, let me make the most important point of all. No one can condemn you or anyone else for owning a trombone and desiring to play it, but performance would be a sin. We love the sinner, but we hate his trombone, don't we? Let's not be misled by those who have openly formed brass bands for performance in the church. You and I will be strong, Craig, and one day the rest of the church will know just what a debt of gratitude they owe us.

Yours in mutual restraint,

Babies and Bathwater

The Protestant Church has thrown out far too many healthy babies in its panic-stricken fear of being polluted by dirty bath water. We have suffered loss and deprivation as a result.

Negative, knee-jerk responses to Mary, the mother of Jesus, have left us with an impoverished appreciation of the female elements of divinity, and an unattractively disrespectful attitude to a very special and heroic lady.

A couple of years ago I took a midnight walk over the Downs with two friends, both from a very low-church background. As we climbed those softly curving, motherly hills beneath the moon, I expressed my view that Mary was regarded slightly neurotically by many evangelical Christians.

People will say things on the Downs at midnight that they might not say anywhere else.

'It's funny you should say that,' said one of my companions, a self-employed builder. 'I was working up on a roof this week with some other blokes, and they were telling jokes and saying things that I just didn't want to hear. And then, suddenly, I felt as if a woman's hands had been placed over my ears.'

We walked on in silence for a moment, then my other friend spoke.

'It *is* funny you should say that. The other day, when I was leading our church meeting, I said something or other about Mary, something sarcastic, I mean, and – I don't know how to describe it – it was as if God slapped me on the wrist. That's how it felt.'

We didn't discuss those experiences any further. There was no point. None of us were about to embrace Rome. We were just opening one or two doors marked 'private'.

Confession is another example. Terrified of being trapped in a box with a man who is trying to do God's job for him, we heedlessly sweep away the entirely scriptural business of confessing our sins to one another. Spiritual and psychological health can sometimes depend on this process.

Often, the baby that we discard grows up elsewhere in a distorted form. Healing goes and Christian Science grows. Spiritual gifts are neglected and a doctrine of 'no salvation without tongues' appears.

Death, and the whole question of communication between heaven and earth, went down the theological waste-pipe a long time ago. These issues are determinedly and consistently prevented from gurgling back to the surface by those sections of the Church whose members have managed to perfect the corporate magic act of concealing fear beneath aggressive or frenetic 'now-ness'. Everyone does it. Last year one of the breakfast programmes spent a week discussing the problem of road accidents involving children. A huge number of kids are killed and injured every year on our roads. Everything was discussed during that week – road safety, careless driving, the evils of drink, proper car maintenance, everything you can think of, except death. Where are all those children who have died? Does it matter? How do we educate our children in an understanding of death? No one seemed to think these questions worth asking.

Spiritualism and absorption in the occult are the mutant and very unwelcome growths that tend to fill the vacuum that is created by this kind of denial in the world and the Church.

Let's hope that we can rescue some of these 'babies', wash the dirty water away and examine them carefully and calmly. Perhaps, then, people like myself, who peep fearfully out from behind the blinds of fear and prejudice, will allow Jesus to shine light into dark corners and amaze us with new and deeper discoveries.

Back to the Future

A couple of years ago we took our bicycles down to Newhaven, crossed by ferry to Northern France, and spent a few enjoyable days pedalling from town to town along the river valleys. Our last day was set aside to explore the port of Dieppe before recrossing the channel that evening.

Just after lunch we entered the cool interior of a big church near the centre of the town. I lost touch with the others for a while, but after a few minutes I discovered Katy, aged four, staring at a life-size sculpture of Mary, the mother of Jesus, holding her son's dead body in her arms and looking into his face with an expression of real pain and loss. Katy turned and saw me.

'Daddy, why has Jesus got a hole in his side?'

Stumblingly, I explained that a Roman spear had been responsible. Katy was horrified. She studied the sculpture again.

'Daddy, he's got holes in his feet. Why has he got holes in his feet?'

'Look,' I pointed to a small crucifix on the wall above us. 'They nailed his feet to that piece of wood called a cross, and those are the holes where the nails were.'

'Nailed his feet?!'

She turned to look at the stone figures again. Her voice broke a little as she spoke.

'Daddy, he's got holes in his hands as well. They didn't nail his hands as well did they?'

Sadly, I explained. Katy moved closer to the sculpture, put her arm around Jesus, and rested her face down on his knee.

Suddenly I longed to go back to the time when I first understood that Jesus died for me and it really hurt, before I covered my faith in words and worries. I wanted to be like a child again.

But I felt like a cabbage.

New to me
But old in years
When he came
Examined tears.
Antique love
Regard me now
Love so good
Kiss my brow.
Complete release
Chance to start
Eventually
Forgive my heart.
Now the peace
Waits for me
Rest in hope
Maybe free.

Book 2:

Clearing Away the Rubbish

*I am indebted to my wife, Bridget,
for preserving what sanity I have
by organizing and editing
the material in this book
with such talent and efficiency.*

Preface

I became a Christian when I was sixteen years old, but it wasn't until I was thirty-seven that I absorbed an essential truth.

God is nice and he likes me.

This seemingly insubstantial fact revolutionized my life. I had juggled with spiritual superlatives and personal guilt for more than twenty years, without experiencing any lasting peace. It wasn't until I underwent emotional disintegration that God was able to reassemble me in a form that was able to perceive and accept the warm gentleness of his care for me.

Why did it take so long? What prevented me, and prevents many others, from finding out about God's love and sense of humour? Who stops us from relaxing in the confidence that we will never be rejected by him?

Over the last few years I have been learning some of the answers to these questions, and trying, through writing and speaking and performing, to pass them on to people who feel weighed down with guilt, and permanently twitchy with sin. Satan is constantly at work piling pieces of convincing-looking rubbish over the truth – anything to prevent us looking at Jesus.

We are all ratbags. None of us is able to reach the level of virtue that would earn us a place in heaven. That's why Jesus died.

This book is a collection of sketches, verse stories, songs, comments and ideas that attempt to expose and remove some of the rubbish that has accumulated over our faith. Please use them in your own situation. They are not exactly literary masterpieces, but if they make people feel a little more free, they'll have done their job.

Reality Is Rotten!

STORIES,
SONGS,
POEMS &
SKETCHES
by Adrian Plass

Christian Confession

Talking about faith in its simplest form has always been a problem to me. I seem to double de-clutch into some strange religious gear that doesn't produce any forward movement at all. I think it has something to do with vocabulary and language habits. A friend of mine, after guest-preaching at a local church, was asked, 'May we fellowship in the petrol?' How did one whole section of the church end up communicating in this strange way? We're all just as bad, whichever denomination we attach ourselves to. We have our own little ways of speaking about and expressing our beliefs and spiritual ideas.

Often this difficulty with language, especially when coupled with a lack of passion, results in a statement of faith that sounds more like a confession of some awful sin than an announcement of salvation and eternal joy. I know. I've done it. I'm working towards being able to ignore the lie that says you can't express your faith in a natural and confident way.

'Christian Confession' requires just two people and a clipboard. The interviewer, armed with his questions, is a typical 'in depth' television reporter. His questions are couched in hushed, empathetic tones as he draws the awful truth from his nervous interviewee. George, twitching and embarrassed, reveals his dependency on Christianity as though he were confessing to drug addiction or sexual perversion. This sketch can be useful for launching discussions, and it really isn't too difficult to do. One of my own particular favourites.

CHRISTIAN CONFESSION

INTERVIEWER: George, you are a Christian?

GEORGE: Yeah, that is true. I am a convicted practisin' Christian.

INTERVIEWER: And how long have you been err ... doing it?

GEORGE: Well, I've been one for a few years now, but I think I was actually one for a little while before that without really realizin' it.

INTERVIEWER: I see. So you weren't always – like you are now?

GEORGE: No, I was a normal kid, grew up like anybody else. Took drugs, got in trouble with the police, pinched stuff from me family and friends, beat a few people up at weekends, owed money all over the place, couldn't handle relationships, scared of the bomb, frightened of cancer, out of work, suicidal, couldn't sleep at night, couldn't stay awake durin' the day, confused about life, terrified of death. I was just your average bloke; I had everythin' goin' for me and I threw it all away.

INTERVIEWER: What happened?

GEORGE: Yeah, well ... there was this party. If I'd known it was a Christian party – I mean, I'd never have gone. I'd always kept away from people like that in the past – Christians I mean. Course, I'd experimented with it. All kids do, don't they? The odd prayer behind the cricket pavilion, a bit of harmless worship with a couple of mates on the way home from school – I mean, it doesn't hurt anyone, does it?

INTERVIEWER: But the party was different?

GEORGE: Yeah ... it was – different.

INTERVIEWER: In what way?

GEORGE: Well, I didn't notice anythin' at first. I was just happily gettin' drunk and makin' a nuisance of myself, like you do at parties, but after a while I suddenly realized that most of the people round me were ... well, I might as well be frank about it – they were sober!

INTERVIEWER: How did that make you feel?

GEORGE: Well, I panicked at first. I mean, it was – it was really *blatant*, know what I mean? And some of them ... they were...

INTERVIEWER: Yes?

GEORGE: They were smilin' at each other.

INTERVIEWER: They were smiling?

GEORGE: Yeah. I really wanted to get out, but someone pushed a tonic water in my hand and I just didn't seem to have any willpower. And then ... then...

INTERVIEWER: Then?

GEORGE: This bloke – must've been a dealer I suppose. He had a load of tracts, and he gave me one, and I – I...

INTERVIEWER: And ...?

GEORGE: I read it.

INTERVIEWER: You – read – a – tract?

GEORGE: Yeah!

INTERVIEWER: And then?

GEORGE: Well, someone pulled the blinds down and we started passin' a New Testament around, and – I dunno – I just couldn't stop. I had to have more and more. I was crazy for it! I met this bloke at midnight behind the dairy the next night, just to pick up a couple of pages of Ezekiel. I was in a terrible state. And then, a few days later, it happened.

INTERVIEWER: What happened?

GEORGE: I – I lost the shakes. My hands stopped shaking. I couldn't make them shake any more, however hard I tried. I started to feel – clean and sort of healthy. I couldn't not sleep at night. I wasn't havin' nightmares. I can't describe it, it was ... awful. But none of that was as bad as when I started...

INTERVIEWER: Go on...

GEORGE: I started bein' ... good!

INTERVIEWER: What form did that take?

GEORGE: Well, it started with little things, you know. I found myself helpin' with the washin' up, passin' things to people without bein' asked – that sort of thing, but then it got worse and worse. I had this awful feelin' that I wasn't the most important person in the world, and people like Max Bygraves had as much right to live as I did...

INTERVIEWER: That's incredible!

GEORGE: I know, I know, but there was nothin' I could do about it! I was on the slippery slope to happiness, and I just didn't know how to stop!

INTERVIEWER: George, what made you do it? What attracted you to Christianity in the first place?

GEORGE: I know what it was! It was the superficial things, the tinselly, glitterin' things that somehow seemed so important.

INTERVIEWER: Such as?

GEORGE: Oh, you know – eternal life, total forgiveness, deep and permanent joy, a chance to find my place in the universe. I was fooled into thinkin' those things were the really important things. The *really* important things, like sex, and money, and power – I dunno, I just lost sight of 'em. You lose your perspective, you see.

INTERVIEWER: And now? Is there hope for you?

GEORGE: Well, I've been away to a – place, and had the err … the cure, and, well, I do feel a bit more hopeful now.

INTERVIEWER: There are some encouraging signs then?

GEORGE: Yes, I'm pleased to say that I *have* been swearin' at my mother – I swore at her a little this mornin' actually – apologized to her afterwards, I'm afraid, but they did say at the – place, that it was bound to take time. I'm hopin' to form a little group over the next few days to beat up people on their way home from church, so … you know, slowly but surely…

INTERVIEWER: George – thank you.

GEORGE: Thank *you*.

Our Times

It takes a lot of courage to describe anything in this book as 'poetry'. On the shelf in front of me as I write are poetry collections by Stewart Henderson and Steve Turner. They are a constant inspiration to me – to write prose. Seriously though, a poem like Stewart's 'A Prophet and a Wet Thursday' is quite enough to remind me of my limitations in this area. In case anyone thinks this is false modesty I'd better add that I'm amazingly good at thousands of other things. I'm one of the slickest light bulb changers in our family, for instance.

I include 'Our Times' for two reasons. First, it provides the reader with an interesting puzzle, and secondly, it illustrates the perils of straying into a field where people are throwing rubbish around in a rather subtle way.

Once, a long time ago, I joined a poetry circle. It met once every month so that members could read their new poems and receive criticism from the rest of the group. I only went twice.

On the first occasion I chickened out of taking any of my poems along. Like many other closet poets, I believed, on the one hand, that my 'works' were probably a load of garbage, but at the same time I nursed a secret fierce hope that they were the product of genius. I didn't feel ready to expose that vulnerable little hope to the possibility of extinction yet, so I decided that for my first visit I would just sit and listen; assess the state of the market, as it were. The poems I heard had two things in common. They were almost totally incomprehensible, and they were just about impossible to respond to. As each one reached its sonorous end, people would either nod mournfully and say 'Mmmm ...' or someone would declare with judicially restrained enthusiasm, 'I think I'd like to hear that again.'

Back at home I studied my own poetry sadly. It was totally flawed by comprehensibility. You could see what it meant at a glance. My only hope was that the members of the poetry circle didn't understand each other's poetry either. But how to test that theory? In the end I decided to take along the piece that I call 'Our Times', read it to the group, and see how they responded. At the next meeting I did exactly that. They were quite impressed, and I never went again.

See if you can guess where 'Our Times' comes from. Clues? Well, it isn't a poem, and there's a strong hint in the title.

OUR TIMES

Like the merchandise of Wells
The wise men state,
Chemical can put up the speed,
In part grassland, in all the fold.
Swirling ooze contains exotic bed of beastly fossil.
Literary corporal garlanded in Ireland,
Luck begins to change for a literary lady.
There's a sign chlorine is included
In nature terminology.
At once correct the tiny slant
Wine drunk to noisy Elsinore accompaniment,
Beetles learning to ride horses,
A plain sort of oyster.*

---

*Did you guess? This 'poem' is the last ten consecutive clues from a *Times* crossword!

Bee

By way of contrast, I wrote this little rhyme when I was a small boy. I know it's a bit silly, but it embodies an acceptance and simplicity that are difficult to recapture as adulthood clamps in. Part of being born again must be the release of that childlike spirit. Perhaps, after a few more years, the Holy Spirit will make me real enough to write something like 'Bee' again!

BEE

The world is very big and round
And in it many things are found
E.g.
A bee.

The Apathetic Creed

Every Sunday in church I say the creed that begins: 'I believe in God the Father ...' Over the years I've learned to understand quite a lot of this awesome statement. I even genuinely mean quite a lot of it. I like to think that when I finally come face-to-face with Jesus the whole thing will flow through me, an explosive rush of ultimate knowledge about the Creator and his creation. In the meantime, an absolutely genuine expression of my creed would be a strange Gruyère-cheese-like version of the original.

I suppose that's true for all of us – believers of different kinds, agnostics, atheists: we've got a personal, idiosyncratic creed, that would look rather strange if it was publicly and honestly revealed.

'The Apathetic Creed' is a light-hearted list/exaggeration of the kinds of unthinking comments often heard from casual opponents of the Christian faith. Hopefully, it encourages Christians to take an honest look at their own *private* creeds. There's nothing wrong with doing that, any more than there's anything wrong with having a look round to see where you've got to in the middle of a journey.

It can be performed by one person, but is possibly more effective when delivered chorally and solemnly by a group. Why not try writing the creeds you might hear from other types of people?

THE APATHETIC CREED

I believe there is something out there,
    but I don't know if I'd call it God, more a sort of
    force.
Anyway you don't have to go to church to be a
    Christian.
What I say is, 'Who made God, anyway?'
What about all the suffering?
What about volcanoes?
And earthquakes.
And floods.
And famines.
And road accidents.
And Ruby Wax.
And depression.
And the bomb.
And cancer.
And AIDS.
And I believe the Bible contradicts itself –
    I don't know exactly where, but it does. It's com-
    mon knowledge.
I rather like what the Buddhists say, or is it the Muslims,
    about getting into a state of real sort of peacefulness.
And I believe it's more important to be a good person
    than to believe in any specific religion,
        and most people who do are fanatics,
        and we all know what fanatics are like.
And I believe people shouldn't be indoctrinated into
    believing things,
        even if they're true.
And I believe that church is very, very boring ...

The Weather

The Weather' is a bit of fun. But it's also a warning not to allow the games we've developed in our churches to obscure the reality that God's love is available in a very simple, uncluttered way.

Unlike some of the pieces in this book, it really does need careful rehearsal, especially the sections where 'responses' are involved.

NB: Weather men change! Don't be afraid to change the sketch accordingly.

THE WEATHER

A group of about ten people are seated on chairs, chatting animatedly as they wait for the meeting to begin. One person is looking self-conscious and unsure. He is here for the first time. After about ten seconds Brother Mervyn, the group leader, enters and takes up a standing position in front of the group. They stop chatting and sit attentively, waiting for him to begin the meeting.

BROTHER MERVYN: Well, good evening, Brothers and
    Sisters, and welcome to tonight's meeting of the

Fifth Day Michael Fishites. *(Holds hand up above his head)* All hail and sleet to Michael Fish!

ALL: *(Fingertips meeting above heads)* May he, with Ian McCaskill and Bill Giles, forecast eternally.

BROTHER MERVYN: May the weather be with you.

ALL: As it was on Wednesday *(lower left hand)* is today *(lower right hand)* and will be on Friday, rain without end, a-gain *(all point forward on second syllable of 'a-gain')*

BROTHER MERVYN: We begin this morning by extending a warm but slightly breezy welcome to our new member, Gregory. *(Gestures towards Gregory)* Doubtless in a bit of a fog at the moment, but you'll soon become acclimatized, Brother Gregory. *(They all titter dutifully)*

SISTER FELICITY: *(Sitting next to Gregory – speaks to him)* Brother Mervyn always says that when we have a new member, Brother Gregory.

BROTHER GREGORY: Oh, does he?

BROTHER MERVYN: Now, over to Sister Meryl for the notices. *(Sits)*

SISTER MERYL: *(Standing and referring to notes)* The 'Sitting on the Beach in Pouring Rain without Umbrellas or Coats Club' will not be meeting next Tuesday as the forecast is for sunshine.

ALL: What a shame! Pity! Nuisance! Oh, dear! *etc.*

SISTER MERYL: As many of you know, Brother Bernard was out on Salisbury Plain last night. He was aiming to prove that, whatever the unmeteorological scoffers may say, it *is* possible to stand in the open in a bucket of water holding twenty pounds of explosives, be struck by lightning, and not only be unharmed, but actually be uplifted by

the experience. We salute him for this great contri-
bution to our cause.

(All applaud enthusiastically)

SISTER FELICITY: What happened?

SISTER MERYL: He's dead.

BROTHER CYRIL: We'll collect some money for him!

SISTER MERYL: We've got to collect *him* first. Finally,
the collection for last week amounted to seventy-
three pence. This will be donated to Brother Stanley, who sustained major damage after excessive
wind on Tuesday night.

(She sits)

BROTHER MERVYN: Thank you, Sister, and now let
us stand and lean for 'Twinkle, Twinkle'. Brother
Ernest, if you please.

*(All stand and lean over to one side. Brother Ernest
beats rhythmically on the glass of a barometer held
in some 'symbolic' fashion. All lean at the end of
each line)*

ALL: *(Singing)* Twinkle, twinkle little star, *(lean)*
We don't wonder what you are, *(lean)*
You're the cooling down of gases, *(lean)*
Forming into solid masses, *(lean)*
Twinkle, twinkle little star, *(lean)*
We don't wonder what you are.

*(All trace a large circle with forefingers, arm
extended fully upwards)*

ALL: *(Slowly and significantly as circles are traced)*
I – so – bars!

(All sit)

BROTHER MERVYN: And now, our reading from the
Outlook according to Fish. *(Raises hand)* May the
clouds part!

185

ALL: *(Stand)* Cumulo Nimbus!

BROTHER MERVYN: Alto Cirrus!

ALL: *(Sit)* Alto Nimbus!

BROTHER MERVYN: Cumulo Cirrus!

ALL: *(Standing)* Thick Fog!

(All sit. Brother Ambrose comes out to read from large book on lectern)

BROTHER AMBROSE: *(In quavering, prophetic tones)* And Michael Fish did prophesy, saying, 'Behold, the heavens shall open and a deluge shall descend,' and it came to pass that no rain fell for many weeks, and they who did till the land did wax wrath against Michael Fish and did revile him, and Michael Fish did speak, saying, 'I can't get it right all the time,' and they did snort and leave him for a season, but those who truly believed wore wellies right through the drought. May Michael Fish be revered.

ALL: With Bill Giles let him be honoured.

BROTHER MERVYN: Yes, indeed. Wonderful words! And now, friends, I'd like us all to greet our new brother, Gregory, here today for the first time.

BROTHER GREGORY: Yes, I saw your postcard in the butcher's.

ALL: *(With pleased significance)* Ah, the postcard! The postcard. Yes, the postcard!

BROTHER MERVYN: Brother Cyril, perhaps you'd introduce Brother Gregory to everyone.

BROTHER CYRIL: Yes, of course. Well, I'm Brother Cyril.

BROTHER GREGORY: Hello.

BROTHER CYRIL: And this is Brother Ernest Hummer.

BROTHER GREGORY: Okay, Ernest?

BROTHER ERNEST: *(Hums earnestly)* Mmmmmm – mmmmmmmm...

BROTHER CYRIL: This is Sister Felicity. She can make a barometer stand up on its hind legs and beg!

BROTHER GREGORY: Really! I'd like to – to see that.

BROTHER CYRIL: You've seen Brother Ambrose, and this is Sister Laetitia. She runs our children's group.

SISTER LAETITIA: We call them 'The Little Drips'.

BROTHER GREGORY: Oh, how nice.

BROTHER MERVYN: Well now, Brother Gregory. Tell us about yourself. You obviously believe deeply in the weather. Is there a particular area that fascinates you?

BROTHER GREGORY: *(Shyly)* Well, I am very blessed by ground temperatures.

BROTHER MERVYN: *(Deeply moved)* Brother Gregory, I believe you have been sent to us for a very special reason. *(Continues in awestruck tones)* Sister Felicity has a special ministry in ground temperatures! *(All react with amazement)*

BROTHER CYRIL: *(He gets a bit excitable sometimes – jumps to his feet and waves his fist in the air)* All hail to the great Michael Fish, for he has done great things! Let the rain fall! Let the lightning flash! Let the thunder roar! Let the wind –

SISTER LAETITIA: Steady, Brother Cyril, that'll do. *(To Brother Gregory)* Brother Cyril is a bit fundamental. But he's so excited about this wonderful link between you and Sister Felicity. Soul mates in the exciting world of ground temperatures!

BROTHER GREGORY: *(Uneasily)* When I say *very* blessed, I don't mean –

SISTER FELICITY: *(With passion)* Brother Gregory, are

187

there any little – problems you'd like to talk about? *(She leans towards him)*

BROTHER GREGORY: Well, I know you're keen on all kinds of weather, and –

SISTER FELICITY: *(She leans even closer)* Yes, indeed!

BROTHER GREGORY: Well, I've often wanted to join a group like this, but ... I hardly know how to say this...

SISTER FELICITY: *(She leans horribly close)* Yes?

BROTHER GREGORY: *(Shame-faced)* Well – I'm afraid I lack humidity.

ALL: Ah! Yes! Mmmmm ... *etc. (Sister Felicity 'comforts' him)*

BROTHER MERVYN: Brother Gregory, believe me when I say that many of us in this room have suffered in this way; some in others. I myself, at one time, was completely unable to accept a deep depression over the Orkneys. For Brother Stanley it is the wind –

BROTHER CYRIL: *(To his feet again)* Ah, the wind, the wind! The wonderful...

BROTHER MERVYN: Sit!

(Brother Cyril sulks)

BROTHER GREGORY: Err ... there was one other thing.

ALL: *(Leaning in unison towards him)* Yes?

BROTHER GREGORY: Well, I wondered how you stand on temperature measurement. I know some groups believe you won't get into the meteorological office unless you measure in Centigrade.

SISTER FELICITY: Brother Gregory, we believe that the important thing is to measure temperature. Some of us do measure it in Centigrade. *(Shyly)* I started one morning quite suddenly a few weeks ago; but some people will always measure in Fahrenheit. That doesn't mean they're not Fishites.

BROTHER MERVYN: We do in fact have a small group who meet every Monday evening just to measure temperature in Centigrade. There's no question of a split.

SISTER LAETITIA: We're all quite calm about it.

BROTHER CYRIL: *(Stands: chants wildly)* Brother Giles we stand with you, freezing point is thirty-two! Fahrenheit is always –

ALL: Sit down! Shuddup! Give it a rest! *etc.*

BROTHER MERVYN: Well, Brother Gregory, we now move into the final part of our meeting. Do you wish to stay?

BROTHER GREGORY: Err ... yes, I suppose so.

BROTHER MERVYN: Very well then. Let us proceed with the ceremony of initiation. Let us stand and affix the blindfolds.

(All stand and put on blindfolds except Brother Gregory)

BROTHER MERVYN: Brother Ernest – if you please!

(Brother Ernest starts his rhythmic tapping on the barometer. They all stand on one leg, extend one hand in front of them, and hop around the stage area hunting for Brother Gregory. As they hop they chant the same words over and over again)

ALL: Seek him! Seek him in the fog! Seek him! Seek him in the fog! *etc.*

(Gregory frantically ducks away from the searching hands, and makes his exit. After a few seconds they too exit, still chanting as they go)

END

Passion Prohibited!

STORIES,
SONGS,
POEMS &
SKETCHES
by Adrian Plass

The Preacher

I first took an interest in the Christian faith when a young
curate, having failed to impress me with rational arguments,
cried, 'I love him! I just love him! I love Jesus!'

It was the passion in his statement that intrigued me. You
can find that same passion in the outpourings of all the bib-
lical characters who walked closely with God. Without this
extravagance of feeling towards God, the Christian religion
is a very unappealing club. It doesn't have to be expressed in
a particular way. Some people use explicit words and movements, others are clearly hugging an immense secret joy within
themselves that spills out in love and care for others.

'The Preacher' was written at a time when this whole issue
had become something of a problem to me. In the situation I
was in I seemed to see more passion and commitment outside
the church than in. I was very arrogant about it – still am probably. The point remains though. Passion pulls people!

THE PREACHER

The preacher stands, his people's rock,
And prays mid walls of stone,
Oh, let my congregation's doubts
Be greater than my own.

I shall not look at Mrs Cook,
For her salvation's won,
But I shall speak to Rosie Cheek,
The whore of Babylon.

For Rosie will not humble me,
Her sins are rich and red,
And seven devils throng her soul,
So Mrs Cook has said.

Oh, Rosie, do not fail me now,
I need you for a while,
I do not ask that you repent,
If you will only smile.

My curate will not smile at me,
I fear he is devout,
I fear he fears I fear that he
Will shortly find me out.

He is a strong yet humble man,
His words are firm but meek,
He bores me to the depths of hell,
God bless you, Rosie Cheek.

I try to love them all, O Lord,
And preach your holy book,
But faith that can move mountains
Would stop short at Mrs Cook.

The preacher sits. Do angels sing?
Have they now what they seek,
Safe in the arms of endless love,
The soul of Rosie Cheek?

For in the lamplit study now,
The coals are burning low,
As cold salvation freezes fast,
The living waters flow.

O Lord, would she have kept her smile
If she had come to me,
And notwithstanding Mrs Cook,
Be closer now to thee?

Salt of the Earth

Salt of the Earth' makes the same point as the last piece. Only an excited appreciation of the way in which Jesus dynamically affects the world can infect others. Books, opinions and theories are no substitute for personal and passionate involvement. It's good to put a bit of welly into the song!

Salt of the Earth

Words and music: Adrian Plass

Words by the mil-lion, books by the ton.__

What a lot of read-ing ev-ery-bo-dy's done!_

How they gon-na know what Je-sus is worth? Well, I

know, know, know, yes, I know

_ he's the salt of the earth.__

Je - sus, Je - sus,

Je - sus is the salt of the earth.__

SALT OF THE EARTH

Words by the million, books by the ton.
What a lot of reading everybody's done!
How they gonna know what Jesus is worth?
Well, I know, know, know,
Yes, I know he's the salt of the earth.
Jesus, Jesus, Jesus is the salt of the earth.

Many people tell me they can only recall
Failure to discover any flavour at all,
I know I'm not exactly spilling over with mirth,
But I know, know, know,
Yes, I know he's the salt of the earth.
Jesus, Jesus, Jesus is the salt of the earth.

Everybody has a little something to say,
You'd think that they were there on resurrection day,
You'd think that they were present at his moment of
    birth,
But do they know, know, know,
Do they know he's the salt of the earth?
Jesus, Jesus, Jesus is the salt of the earth.

God is in his heaven, is his heaven in you?
Can you hear him saying what he wants you to do?
Jesus is the one and only way to rebirth,
And then you, you, you,
Yes, you will be the salt of the earth.
Yes, you, you, you, oh, you will be the salt of the earth,
Jesus, Jesus, Jesus is the salt of the earth.

Promote Party Spirit!

STORIES,
SONGS,
POEMS &
SKETCHES
by Adrian Plass

Hallelujah in the Back of My Mind

I don't mind denominations. In fact, I like them really. It's always good to have a variety of flavours available, and it's not a bad thing to educate your tastebuds with the odd sip at a concoction you've never tried. A local pastor said at a (genuinely) ecumenical meeting recently that if we have real love for each other as followers of Jesus, then we have the only kind of unity that really matters. I think he's right, although that 'if' can be a rather large one sometimes.

From the unchurched person's point of view though, it must all be a bit confusing, especially if he or she encounters one of those church-hopping individuals who is constantly leaving a fellowship or church because of some obscure piece of 'totally unacceptable' dogma, never pausing to reflect that his inability to settle might be something to do with *him*. I think I was a bit like that – over-critical and judgemental. It was a great relief to discover eventually that a simple commitment to one church, and a willingness to accept that church in the same way that God accepts me, was the antidote to that kind of restlessness.

During a period of nearly two years when we didn't attend any church, however, I got pretty fed up with *all* the denominations, and wrote the words of 'Hallelujah in the Back of My Mind' as an expression of my frustration. It was also a cry of relief that God stayed with me when the church institutions seemed so uninviting. I can still sing or read the words with real feeling, but I have to add that, in my view, denominational differences can be yet another devilish red herring – or dead kipper.

The message is all in the words, so there's no point in bashing through too quickly. When I read it as verse, I usually leave out all but the final chorus, otherwise it lasts for about three weeks ... James Hammond even wrote the tune for this one.

Hallelujah in the Back of My Mind

Words: Adrian Plass
Music: James Hammond

I take my prob-lems to the al-tar, but my
real-ly want to share it, but I

steps be-gin to fal-ter and I feel as if I'm start-ing to fall,
know they'll ne-ver wear it, and the ques-tion in my head is un-der-

— for it's hard to re-col-lect the pro-per
-lined. But just as I am say-ing, 'Who on

way to ge-nu-flect up-on ar-ri-val in a Pen-te-cos-tal
earth in-vent-ed pray-ing?' Hal-le-lu-jah in the back of my—

1. hall. And I
2. mind. Hal-le-lu-jah in the

CHORUS

back of my mind, hal-le-lu-jah in the back of my mind,

— I've got to hand it

to you, Lord, you're real-ly com-ing through, with hal-le-

-lu-jah in the back of my mind.

HALLELUJAH IN THE BACK OF MY MIND

I take my problems to the altar, but my steps begin to
    falter
And I feel as if I'm starting to fall,
For it's hard to recollect the proper way to genuflect,
Upon arrival in a Pentecostal hall.
And I really want to share it, but I know they'll never
    wear it,
And the question in my head is underlined.
But just as I am saying, 'Who on earth invented
    praying?'
Hallelujah in the back of my mind.

Chorus:
    Hallelujah in the back of my mind,
    Hallelujah in the back of my mind,
    I've got to hand it to you, Lord,
    You're really coming through,
    With hallelujah in the back of my mind.

There are some who have you kneeling, there are those
    who hit the ceiling,
There are others who insist on a smell,
There are some who keep their hats on, and a very few
    are bats on
Having serpents in the service as well.
There are those who call you 'sinner' if you dare enjoy
    your dinner,
And Gomorrah's in a half a glass of wine,
But just as I am sure I can't survive it any more,
Hallelujah in the back of my mind.

Well, they say, 'Oh yes you may do what you feel
    because it's real,
And everybody must be perfectly free,
And I'm happy to advise you not a soul will criticise
    you,
Just as long as you are copying me.'
So I take it and I shake it and I really try to break it,
And I think I'm gonna leave it behind,
But just as I've dismissed it, there's a sound, I can't
    resist it,
Hallelujah in the back of my mind.

Chorus:
    Hallelujah ... *etc.*

There's a man who when I'm sickly, says, 'You very,
    very quickly
Should be starting to be better, not worse,'
And he tells me that he sees I'm needing longer on my
    knees,
And there will always be a relevant verse.
But some say if you suffer,
then your spirit will get tougher,
So you'd better find a will and get it signed,
But just as I'm refusing to go on, it's so confusing,
Hallelujah in the back of my mind.

Chorus:
    Hallelujah ... *etc.*

There are many, many people who rely upon a steeple,
To remind them that they're aiming at God,

While some discover Zion under corrugated iron,
And they none of them believe they are odd,
For they know the congregation in their own
    denomination
Is the nearest thing to heaven you can find,
But when I say, 'That's it! O Lord, I know I'll never fit,'
Hallelujah in the back of my mind.

Chorus:
   Hallelujah in the back of my mind,
   Hallelujah in the back of my mind,
   I've got to hand it to you, Lord,
   You're really coming through,
   With hallelujah in the back of my mind.

Anagrams

Problems can arise from denominational differences when a particular group or church or fellowship seizes on one detail or aspect of religious activity and majors on it to such an extent that the really vital things become relatively unimportant. A man stands under an apple tree. Five apples hit him on the head. As the fifth one strikes he has a divine revelation. Before long 'The Church of the Fifth Apple' is planted. Every Sunday fruit figures heavily in the order of service. A bit of an exaggeration? Well, yes ... perhaps, but you know what I mean.

Readers of *The Sacred Diary* can't have failed to become aware that I used to be keen on working out anagrams for the names of famous Christians and politicians. One or two earnest folk have said to me, 'You know, there's more in these anagrams than meets the eye.' Noting the gleam in their eye that suggests they are about to found the 'Church of the Fifteenth Anagram', I always hasten to assure them that it's just a bit of fun. But those comments set me thinking. What might the equivalent of the Anglican Lesson sound like in the 'Church of the Fifteenth Anagram'?

The piece entitled 'Anagrams' hopefully makes the point about undue emphasis, but it's also an opportunity to say one or two serious things in the midst of humour. The 'congregation' can be as small as two, or even one, if volunteers are scarce. I often leave out the response sections and do it as a one-man reading. The voice needs to be that of your average stage vicar, evening out into normal tones for the final more serious sections.

Since this book first appeared, many of the names in this piece have become out of date. I've left it as it was, though, a sort of verbal fossil! Do substitute any names you want to.

ANAGRAMS

READER: The first lesson is taken from the second book of Anagrams, chapter five, verse sixteen, beginning at Ronald Reagan. May our names be unchanged!

CONGREGATION: (*in flat unison*) Sock it to us, Julie.

READER: May we never suffer rearrangement!

CONGREGATION: We do not know what you are talking about, Bernard.

READER: May our letters stay intact!

CONGREGATION: If you don't get on with it, Myrtle, we shall come up there and rearrange your liver.

READER: Two Anagrams, chapter five, verse sixteen. And Ronald Reagan was an anagram of 'An oral danger'.

And David Steel was an anagram of 'Vital deeds', and 'Slated dive'.

And David Owen was an anagram of 'An odd view', and 'A dive down', and 'Dawn video'.

And Neil Kinnock was an anagram of 'I know Lenin'.

And Maggie Thatcher ...

(*All kneel*)

was an anagram of 'Get rich team hag'.

And Norman Tebbit was an anagram of 'Ointment barb', and 'Mor'n a bit bent'.

And Enoch Powell was an anagram of 'One we'll chop'.

And Max Bygraves was an anagram of 'Marvy sex-bag'.

And Alvin Stardust was an anagram of 'I trust vandals'.

And Elvis Presley was an anagram of 'Silvery Sleep'.

And Barry Manilow was an anagram of 'Woman Library'.

And love ...

(All stand)

CONGREGATION: *(like a sighing wind)* Yes ...?

READER: ... is an anagram of 'Vole',
And lost love ...

CONGREGATION: Is an anagram of ...?

READER: 'Vole slot'

(Boldly) And Robert Runcie is an anagram of 'C.E. but in error'

And 'Ice-bun terror'.

And Billy Graham is an anagram of 'Big rally ham'.

And mother-in-law is an anagram of 'Woman Hitler'.

And Mother Theresa is an anagram of 'Heart rest-home'.

(Pause)

And security is an anagram of 'Rusty ice'.

(All take up the sss ... of 'ice')

And sweat is an anagram of 'Waste',
And close friend is an anagram of 'Closer fiend'.

And forgiveness is an anagram of 'Serving foes'.

And apartheid is an anagram of 'Death pair'.

READER AND CONGREGATION: 'A dire path'

'A heart dip'

'A dirt heap'

READER: A death rip.

And tomorrow is an anagram of 'Root worm'.

And today is an anagram of 'Toady'.

And yesterday...

(Member of congregation sings) 'All my troubles seemed so far away ...'

(He is quickly extinguished)

READER: Yesterday is an anagram of 'A seedy try'.

A nuclear bomb is an anagram of 'Rub once balm'.

And utter despair is an anagram of 'Rutted praise'.

And Armageddon is an anagram of 'An armed God'.

Here ends the lesson.

(Pause)

VOICE: Lord, in thy mercy ...

READER AND CONGREGATION: ... hear our prayer.

The Well

The Well' is a parable, so in the best tradition of parable tell-ers I shall let it speak for itself.

THE WELL

Once upon a time a rich landowner built a village and invited people to come and live in it. He pointed out that a well had been sunk in the centre of the village square, and being a good man, he was particularly anxious to make it clear that each villager, however humble, had an equal right to draw water at any time and in any quantity he or she wished, especially as there was no other water source available. He then set off on his travels, confident that all would be in harmony when he returned in the distant future.

For a time the villagers used the well as the land-owner had intended, but gradually things changed. The richer and more socially prominent citizens began to feel annoyed that the humbler element in the village were able to keep *them* waiting in a queue. It didn't seem right. They solved the problem by creating new village laws about access to the well. Water could only be obtained at certain set times and in certain set quantities. Moreover, two long forms had to be filled in on each occasion, and water was only to be drawn by a hireling of the rich faction. Not only did this solve the queue problem, it also deterred the poorer villagers from applying for water even at the set times. The forms were very long and complicated. They preferred to make do on less water. The rich group on the other hand, being better educated and more highly motivated towards the written word, were very happy indeed with the arrangement. The change in the law they justified by claiming that a document had been discovered written by the landowner, and instructing them to proceed in this way.

Time passed.

Some years later an intelligent and very vocal young man announced that he had been elected as a representative of the poor people of the village in matters pertaining to water. Furthermore, he informed the ruling group, he too had discovered a document written by the landowner, in which it was stated absolutely clearly that it was quite unnecessary to fill in forms to obtain water. Instead, each villager was to perform a certain sequence of dance steps if he or she wanted access to the well. The details of the dance, he claimed, were contained in the document.

They demanded to see his document. He demanded to see theirs. No documents appeared.

Fearing the vocal young man's capacity for inciting rebellion, the rich faction decided to allow the 'dance-step' method of obtaining water for the poorer citizens, while continuing with the form-filling method themselves.

There were now two official drawers of water posted at the well. One inspected forms and supplied water at set times if the forms were completed correctly, the other studied the execution of the prescribed dance and responded accordingly. Newcomers to the village were obliged to adopt one of these methods for obtaining water, as there was no other source. Occasionally, a villager might change from being a form-filler to being a dancer, or the other way round, but not very often.

As the years passed no one could quite remember the origin of these differences, but as it worked reasonably well, it didn't seem to matter. The only problem was that it did get a bit crowded round the well at times.

Eventually, the landowner returned to the village unexpectedly. Coming up to the well, he was greeted by the two official drawers of water, who asked him if he wished to fill in forms or do the dance. Bewildered, he asked them what they meant. They explained that, as far as they knew, the person who built the village in the first place had laid down a law that water was only to be given to dancers or form-fillers. They were hoping, they added, that the owner of the village would return soon, so that they could persuade him to provide a second well. That would make things so much clearer and more convenient.

The landowner wept.

Misery Is Manifold!

STORIES,
SONGS,
POEMS &
SKETCHES
by Adrian Plass

Growbag World

I wrote 'Growbag World' in response to a picture painted by a very close friend of mine. As I sat alone, gazing at his painting of teazles reaching up towards a fragmented moon in an ominously leaden sky, I made rough notes about my immediate reaction to the picture. Later, at home, I wrote a set of verses loosely based on those notes. As the poem progressed, I realised that I was writing more about my friend than about his painting. He is a church leader, an enabler and encourager of others. Over the years thousands of people must have benefited from his consistent warmth and ability to listen without judging and confining. I don't mean that he's flawless. He would laugh at the very idea. I don't think we protect and care for our good church leaders as we should. It's so comfortable to assume that at least *one* person is strong and safe and sound. Actually, the cost of being a public optimist can be enormous. There can be only one hero in the book of any Christian's life, and that's God. The tendency to lean too heavily on individual Christian leaders can be a postponement of real contact with God.

GROWBAG WORLD

Upon this giant growbag world,
I planted seeds of light

And dreamed a glowing harvest,
That would penetrate the night.

But as I toiled upon my knees,
They ringed me round with gloom,
Their pockets full of pallid hands,
Their voices full of doom.

'We tell the truth, the truth is dark,
There is no light to save,
Your seeds will never break the earth,
Your garden is a grave.'

And yet I work, I work, I work,
And now my seeds have grown,
I touch the cold and lightless leaves,
And love them as my own.

And will there come a morning soon,
When flowers from the shade,
Will bloom and break, and float, and light
The world that you have made?

How hard, how hard, to paint a dream,
For eyes that cannot shine,
For eyes too dulled by twilight skies,
To see the dawn in mine.

Poison Pools

Sin can be very attractive, especially if the alternatives appear joyless and full of strain. Why try, if trying looks more like gloom than glory? That's how I felt when I wrote 'Poison Pools'. I try to remember that feeling now when I meet Christians who are low. Jesus came down to rescue us. Let's go down to rescue our brothers and sisters, then we can climb back up together. Someone did that for me.

POISON POOLS

Who made these poison pools
In desert lands?
So sweet and cool,
A welcome lie,
The chance to die with water on my lips.
I've seen how others try to die unpoisoned in the sun.
I do not think that I can do as they have done.

Shell

I wrote this book as I was approaching forty. The previous four years of my life had probably been the most satisfying I'd known.

I hated becoming thirty. I wrote this poem on August the fourth, nineteen seventy-eight. It's how I felt, and I'm glad it's there as a record, or a yardstick, or something. It's a part of my shadow that's better out than in…

SHELL

Saw a shell
Rich with mother-of-pearl.
Waited
So long
To see the creature that needed such delicate protection.
Realised
So late
The creature was long gone.
Soaked with sea,
Drifting in heaven or hell,
But certainly
Not minding.

When Does the Joy Start?

Why do so many Christians ask this question? Like disappointed children they can't understand why the promises don't seem to be kept. Especially, perhaps, they have great difficulty in believing that God really loves *them*. How gratifying for the devil to see how this most basic truth and reassurance is denied to many who want to follow Jesus. Only love will reveal love – not slick answers.

I wrote 'When Does the Joy Start?' when I needed answers myself.

When Does the Joy Start?

Words and music: Adrian Plass

The light I have is slowly fading, there's no sign of a change. Tell me, why is this darkness so sweet and so strange? Did I think you were joking? Did I think you were mad when you told me to follow the good and the bad? When does the joy start? When do the clouds part? When does the dawn break? When does the earth shake? When does the choir sing? When do the bells ring? When will I rise with him?

WHEN DOES THE JOY START?

The light I have is slowly fading,
There's no sign of a change.
Tell me, why is this darkness
So sweet and so strange?
Did I think you were joking?
Did I think you were mad
When you told me to follow
The good and the bad?

When does the joy start?
When do the clouds part?
When does the dawn break?
When does the earth shake?
When does the choir sing?
When do the bells ring?
When will I rise with him?

My friends all say I should be leaving,
It may be true that I'm slow.
If you know me like they do,
Do you still want to know?
If I knew where to head for,
I would certainly go;
I need someone to tell me,
And you seem to know.

So when does the joy start?
When do the clouds part?
When does the dawn break?
When does the earth shake?
When does the choir sing?
When do the bells ring?
When will I rise with him?

I shall not move until you bless me,
I will stand by your door.
In your moment of leaving
You will see me, I'm sure.
All I need is a moment,
All I ask is a smile,
Just to know that you love me,
That'll do for a while.

And that's when the joy starts,
That's when the clouds part,
That's when the dawn breaks,
That's when the earth shakes,
That's when the choir sings,
That's when the bells ring,
That's when I rise with him.

That's when you'll see me,
That's when you'll free me,
That's when my star falls,
That's when my God calls,
Calls out to my heart,
That's when the joy starts,
That's when I rise with him.

Perfection Is Possible!

STORIES,
SONGS,
POEMS &
SKETCHES
by Adrian Plass

The Law

I once made a television programme with Peter Ball when he was the bishop of Lewes. As we stood in near darkness at one end of the studio waiting for the floor manager to call us onto the set, someone asked Peter how sure he was about some aspect of Christian doctrine. Dear Peter gives just about everything he's got in every waking hour, but on this particular morning he was very low.

'The only thing I'm sure of at the moment,' he said quietly, 'is that I'm a sinner.'

Fortunately, Peter knew and still knows that God is always willing and able to forgive him. He has practised being forgiven for years. That doesn't mean it's invariably easy, but it does mean that, in a very real sense, hope springs eternal.

Most of us can identify with the feeling that our sin is the only thing we're sure about. The problems come when forgiveness is not a corresponding or balancing fact of life. For years I laboured under the delusion that I needed to earn my way into God's good books. I knew the theology, but I wasn't convinced. The result was a sort of superficial, arid virtue, bloodless and boring. Sin continued of course, but even the sin wasn't very interesting. So many people I meet are still trying to live according to law. We can't do it. Jesus died *because* we can't do it. We only have to be conscious for a few seconds each morning to know that the law is too much for us. That knowledge, properly understood, can be the beginning of freedom.

'The Law' is, again, a simple piece of verse, but it repays careful rehearsal by the two participants. Wigs and gowns add a lot, but aren't essential. A fairly sharp contrast between the personalities of Murgatroyd and Pratt is an aid to effectiveness. Above all – enjoy it! The two lawyers rather relish the hopelessness of their message.

THE LAW

MURGATROYD: We have a feeling some of you
　　Are feeling fairly sure
　　That all you really need to do
　　Is try to keep the law.
PRATT: You wish you knew for sure, though,
　　Can you break it once or twice,
　　And still get into heaven?
　　What you need is some advice.
MURGATROYD: You need some legal expertise,
　　And we provide just that,
　　We are your humble servants
　　Messrs Murgatroyd…
PRATT: And Pratt.
MURGATROYD: The law is rather difficult,
PRATT: There's such a lot of it,
MURGATROYD: Perhaps you haven't understood.
PRATT: Perhaps you are a twit.
MURGATROYD: If you decide to live by law
PRATT: You'd better heed our warning,
MURGATROYD: The first mistake that you will make
PRATT: Is waking in the morning.
MURGATROYD: The moment the alarm has gone
PRATT: You'll make a tiny slip,

MURGATROYD: And by the time you're out of bed,

PRATT: You're in the devil's grip!

MURGATROYD: You can't be bad,

PRATT: Or sad

MURGATROYD: Or mad

PRATT: Or rude

MURGATROYD: Or crude

PRATT: Or greedy.

MURGATROYD: You're not allowed to flash

PRATT: Your cash (holds up wads of notes)

MURGATROYD: You give it to the needy. *(Takes cash from Pratt)*

MURGATROYD: You aren't allowed

PRATT: To shun the crowd,

MURGATROYD: You've got to love them all,

PRATT: Especially if

MURGATROYD: They bore you stiff

PRATT: And drive you up the wall.

MURGATROYD: You mustn't steal

PRATT: Or fight

MURGATROYD: Or feel

PRATT: Embarrassed by your zits

MURGATROYD: Or go along to swimming pools

PRATT: To look at naughty bits.

MURGATROYD: Can you forgive your cousin, Viv,

PRATT: And tell her so as well?

MURGATROYD: And stay with ancient Auntie May

PRATT: Despite the horrid smell?

MURGATROYD: And if you're lending anything

PRATT: That you will sadly miss,

MURGATROYD: You're not allowed to want it back,

PRATT: For instance – lend me this? *(Takes back cash)*

MURGATROYD: And if you *do* do something right

229

PRATT: It's no good saying, 'Well!'

PRATT AND MURGATROYD: I *am* a little sunbeam
   now – !

MURGATROYD: That's pride,

PRATT: You'll go to hell.

MURGATROYD: We hope we have conveyed to you

PRATT: The danger you are in,

MURGATROYD: But please, you mustn't worry,

PRATT: No you mustn't, it's a sin.

MURGATROYD: You see, you'll never keep the law,

PRATT: There's not a chance of that.

MURGATROYD: We promise you can take the word – of
   Murgatroyd

PRATT: And Pratt.

I Found a Bird

One of the greatest barriers to prayer in my life has been an obsession with self-image. I never wanted to let God in through the front door of my life until I'd tidied up all the messes, done the washing-up, cleaned the windows and made the beds. Never realizing how gladly and joyfully he would have come in, rolled his sleeves up and given me a hand, I kept him waiting outside while I tried to do an impossibly perfect job on my own. Ironically, it wasn't until I hit rock-bottom that I realized how all that stuff about God loving me whatever happened was true. In the darkest and most difficult times Jesus was there – sometimes in the most unlikely situations. He wasn't ashamed to be with me, just as he wasn't ashamed to be with publicans and sinners two thousand years ago.

Nowadays, I tend to leave the door on the latch.

'I Found a Bird' is from those dark days. Best sung without accompaniment if you have the courage. I don't very often.

I Found a Bird

Words and music: Adrian Plass

I found a bird with a bro-ken wing.

When she knew that I loved her ___ she be-gan to sing.

Did you ev-er lose some-one? Have you ev-er felt blue?

If you ev-er go down there, he's there with you.

I FOUND A BIRD

I found a bird with a broken wing.
When she knew that I loved her
She began to sing.
Did you ever lose someone?
Have you ever felt blue?
If you ever go down there,
He's there with you.

I know a bar, where my wild time blows.
There's a tune on the juke-box,
Sad as a rose.
Have you ever been down there?
Have you ever been blue?
If you ever go down there,
He's there with you.

Then you find a road, seems to lead somewhere.
They say you'll go a long way
On a wing and a prayer,
But did you ever just wonder,
Why you still feel blue?
If you ever go down there,
He's there with you.

Whoever made days, didn't make them right,
'Cause the days keep changing
Into weeping nights.
Have you ever been lonely?
Have you ever been blue?
If you ever go down there,
He's there with you.

We all gotta change the way that we are.
Every last one of us
Gonna find a star.
But if you ever grow weary,
If you ever just feel blue,
If you ever go down there,
He's there with you.

I Didn't Have to See You

'I Didn't Have to See You' was born during a period when I was recovering from illness, and it records a growing awareness that the way I feel, physically, emotionally or spiritually, has little to do with God's ever-present love and faithfulness. That sounds all very wonderful of course, but I very frequently have a job remembering it. One of his infernal majesty's most effective pieces of rubbish!

This one is meant to be sung to the tune of Paul Winter's 'I Didn't Have to See You'.

I DIDN'T HAVE TO SEE YOU

I didn't have to see you
In the night-time, there by the side of me.
I knew it had to be you,
Knew you loved the child inside of me.
You smiled in the darkness,
It seemed to blind and burn,
But when my eyes were opened,
I smiled in return, for you were there.

I didn't have to hear you
In the silence, you were a part of me,
I knew that I was near you,

Knew your love was deep in the heart of me,
I knew that you were saying,
Our happiness has grown,
For prayer is only friendship,
You never were alone, for I was there.

I didn't have to hold you,
I was trusting, knowing your care for me,
The secrets I had told you,
Knowing you would always be there for me,
So let the darkness gather,
And let the silence roll,
The love that made you suffer,
Is glowing in my soul, and you are there.

Callous Creator!

STORIES,
SONGS,
POEMS &
SKETCHES
by Adrian Plass

My Baby

I have to confess that, as clay goes, I'm not very good at accepting everything the Potter says and does without question. I have often come to a frowning halt while reading Scripture, my twittering finite mind unable to proceed because something God has said or done 'isn't fair', or 'doesn't make sense'. Part of me likes the fact that some questions are unanswerable – one of the best pieces of advice I was ever given was, 'Learn to live in the mystery' – but another part of me moans and grunts and huffs at the prospect of simply accepting apparently unacceptable truths. God forgives me, irksome though I am, and even, very occasionally, provides aids to acceptance. 'My Baby' is one of those.

When I was working on the narration side of David and Bathsheba (see 'Nathan Rap' pre-amble), I came to one of those full stops of non-acceptance when I read about the death of David's son, the baby born out of David's illicit union with Bathsheba. The Bible states quite categorically that God caused the baby to fall sick and die as a specific punishment for David's crimes of adultery and murder. I found myself unable to carry on with the narrative because an overwhelming question blocked the way.

Why? Why did God kill the baby? *How* could he?

Traditional answers were no use to me. I knew them – had used them to answer others. They sprang to mind with Pavlovian ease. None of them allowed me to go on writing. David, I was interested to note, was able to accept the death of his child, not without grief, but without a trace of anger or resentment.

I couldn't accept it.

Then one afternoon, as I was walking the half-mile or so to collect my sons from junior school, a procession of words marched through my brain. When I got home I wrote them down, and soon the narrative was complete. It's not *the* answer. It's *an* answer – my answer, but I think others might find it helpful. One of the devil's most successful deceptions is the one about God standing aloof and detached from human suffering. He knows how it feels, and he shares in it.

MY BABY

I wish you knew how much I love you all. I wish you could trust me in the way that David did. You've asked me a question about the death of a baby. Now I will ask *you* some questions, and you must decide whether I've earned the right to be trusted whatever I do. My questions are about Jesus.

When he was dragged from the garden of Gethsemane after a night of agonised prayer and terrible, lonely fear; when he was put on trial simply for being himself, and beaten, and kicked, and jeered at; did I insist that you solve for me the problem of pain? I let you hurt and abuse my son – my baby.

When he hauled himself, bruised and bleeding along the road to his own death, knowing that a single word from him would be enough to make me release him from his burden, did I let you down? No, I let you crush him under the weight of your cross. My son – my baby.

240

And when the first nail smashed into the palm of his hand, and everything in my father's heart wanted to say to those legions of weeping angels, 'Go! Fight your way through and rescue him. Bring him back where he belongs,' did I abandon you to judgement? No, I let you kill my son – my baby.

And when he had been up on that accursed cross for three long hours, and with every ounce of strength left in his poor suffering body, he screamed at *me*, 'Why have you forsaken me?' did I scream back, 'I haven't! I haven't! It's all just a nightmare – come back, they aren't worth it!'

No, I loved you too much – far too much to do that. I let your sin cut me off from my son – my baby.

And that death, dismal, depressing and horribly unjust as it was – the death of my innocent son, has brought peace and life to millions who've followed the same Jesus, who came back to life, back to his friends, and back to me.

Trust me. When it comes to the death of babies – believe me – I do know what I'm doing.

Why Did He Choose ...?

It was through reading Malcolm Muggeridge's comments on the life of Jesus that I came to realize how vividly alive the Son of God was as a human being. Jesus loved nature (referring to natural beauty often in the Gospels), people generally, his friends in particular, the cut and thrust of debate and argument, in fact the whole rich business of being alive. There must have been times when he quietly mused over what might have been, if it had been possible to avoid the path of obedience to the cross.

Why Did He Choose . . . ?

Words and music: Adrian Plass

What a moun-tain climb-er___ this Je-sus might have been! Climb-ing through the sha-dows of the sca-ri - est ra - vine, com-ing through and rest-ing where the air is cold and clean, what a moun-tain climb-er this Je-sus might have been!___ So why did he choose___

CHORUS

death on a hill - side, a-go-ny un - der a mer-ci-less sky?___ When he could have stayed home, could have played with the thun - der. Was I real-ly the rea - son he de-ci-ded to die?

WHY DID HE CHOOSE ... ?

What a mountain climber this Jesus might have been!
Climbing through the shadows of the scariest ravine,
Coming through and resting where the air is cold and
    clean,
What a mountain climber this Jesus might have been.

Chorus:
> So why did he choose death on a hillside,
> Agony under a merciless sky?
> When he could have stayed home,
> Could have played with the thunder.
> Was I really the reason he decided to die?

What a disco dancer this Jesus might have been,
Moving sweetly on the Galilean disco scene,
Dancing like a fire through the red and gold and green,
What a disco dancer this Jesus might have been.

Chorus:
> So why ... *etc.*

What a famous lover this Jesus might have been,
Up there with the others on the giant silver screen,
Showing all the ladies what a kiss could really mean,
What a famous lover this Jesus might have been.

Chorus:
> So why ... *etc.*

What a leg-spin bowler this Jesus might have been,
A holy Rowley Jenkins on some Jewish village green,
Curling like a snake, and taking five for seventeen,
What a leg-spin bowler this Jesus might have been.

Chorus:
So why ... *etc.*

What a loving father this Jesus might have been,
Walking by his lady with the children in between,
Something in their faces that I have never seen,
What a loving father this Jesus might have been.

Chorus:
So why ... *etc.*

Letter to God – and God's Reply

One of the things that must have been particularly fascinating for those who followed Jesus through his three-year ministry on earth, was the amazing variety and ingenuity of his approach to people and situations. Take healing for instance. One person, a deaf man, is taken to a quiet place outside the city to receive his healing. (There are obvious practical reasons for that of course.) Another, the man with the withered hand, is placed in front of an entire congregation and publicly healed for a completely different set of very good reasons. The disciples must have lived in a state of constant anticipation. Tax paid with a coin found in a fish's mouth, walking on the water, five thousand fed with one packed lunch – what next?

Bearing all this in mind, it seems strange and sad that the church is so frequently found to be unimaginative and stolidly cautious in its approach to most things. For this reason, perhaps, I always used to feel a vague sense of guilt about using 'devices' in my own relationship with God. This was greatly eased when one such device produced unexpected results.

I had written a letter to God, a prayer on paper if you like, and I read it out one night on the TVS epilogue programme *Company*. Imagine my surprise, a couple of days later, when I received a reply to my letter in the post, signed 'God'. What follows is the letter and the reply, together with a small but important explanatory footnote.

246

I often read these letters to groups or congregations, partly because it was an interesting and moving sequence of events, and partly to encourage others to use whatever novel means of prayer or worship might occur to them.

God is accessible, and he does want to hear from us.

LETTER TO GOD...

Dear God,

First of all, I'm sorry it's so long since I last wrote. I realize that postcards are a bit of a cop-out, but to be honest I've just had too much that I either had to do, or wanted to do, more than settle down and let you know just how things are. I do think about you quite a lot though, and I'm ashamed to say I often pretend to others that I'm in more regular contact with you than I really am.

'Oh yes,' I say, 'God and I are just like that. I don't know what I'd do if he wasn't constantly advising me on everything; and,' I add, 'he's very fond of me of course.'

Actually, that's one of the reasons I've got down to writing to you at last. You see, although I say that to people, and although part of me is sure it's true, sometimes I think I must be round the bend just thinking it. You see, the trouble is – you're not actually here, and every now and then I panic, and everything goes dark and empty, and the life drains out of anything good, and there seem to be only shadows.

I sometimes think back to those telephone conversations we used to have – when I was writing to you every day – do you remember? I used to get really excited waiting for the phone to go...

Why isn't it like that any more?

I suppose what I'm really saying is, despite the fact that I haven't done much to keep in touch lately, I still want to know that you and me are ... well, that you are still interested in me.

I'd better confess, by the way, that most of those postcards I sent I wrote in advance, and just sent one every now and then.

So ... I really haven't done very well, have I? And I wouldn't blame you if you didn't answer this letter. In fact, I don't know why you seemed so taken with me in the first place. People I knew said that it was because you didn't really know me, and that I was a 'big-head' to think that you had any time for ordinary people like me. But what they don't know is about all those things I told you about myself – some of them I've never told anyone else. Also, none of them knew how after a long time of nobody speaking, and me thinking you'd put the phone down because you were so disgusted, you said, 'I knew all about that before we met, and it makes no difference.'

And I said, 'Why not?'

And you said, 'Because I love you.'

Well, I suppose I want to get back to the way I felt then, and I've been reading all your old letters over and over again. It's almost like having you here in the room.

Now that I've written properly, please call me – soon.

I'll be waiting to hear from you.

Love,
Adrian

Dear Adrian,

I was so glad to receive your letter at last, and to know that you still think about me. I thought this was better than a phone call, and of course I am sending this message through someone whom I trust, and who has great faith. I do hope you have been able to clear your mind in those areas that needed clearing, and I also want to let you know that *I* think of *you* all the time.

There are so many I have to share my love with, and so many find it difficult to express themselves. Others find it easier. I know people have great difficulties in praying, but to me *any* communication is better than nothing. Don't forget, Adrian, that I am always listening – and it's so simple really. Just speak from the heart.

You won't forget to communicate again, will you? I'll look forward to it.

My love is with you always,
God

NB: Close examination of the handwriting revealed that the letter was actually written by my mother. Later I learned that she had been up late one night and seen the broadcast in which I read my letter to God. She felt that God wanted her to convey his reply to me. I believe she was right.

Feeling Is Failing!

STORIES,
SONGS,
POEMS &
SKETCHES
by Adrian Plass

Hall of Mirrors *and* When I Was a Small Boy

Most of my adult life has been spent working with disturbed children in a variety of settings. In the process I probably learned more about myself than anything else, but some things became clear. For instance, I realized eventually that most of the children I met in boarding schools for the maladjusted, assessment centres, and secure units had one problem in common. They needed to know who and what they were. It wasn't easy for them because there was more than one answer available to the question they were constantly (if unconsciously) asking. It was rather like standing in one of those halls of distorting mirrors. The child's own family flung one reflection back at him, the staff in his residential establishment another, the dreaded 'file' yet another, and then there were friends, the police perhaps, one or more sets of foster parents, and his own social worker, a figure who was supposed to provide consistency but might actually change with bewildering frequency.

'Hall of Mirrors' was a simple and certainly inadequate expression of this particular problem, but I was interested much later on, when I left residential social work because of my own emotional problems, to see how these few lines summed up the problems I was experiencing with my *spiritual* identity. What were the distorting mirrors that prevented me from seeing God clearly? This book is full of them.

How about you?

'When I Was a Small Boy' is a record of my own rather pessimistic fear that the wounds of childhood can never really be healed. The poem is now largely out of date, thank God.

HALL OF MIRRORS

Stranded in the hall of mirrors
I must struggle to avoid
Images that cannot show me
Something long ago destroyed.

In the darkness, in the distance
In a corner of my mind,
Stands a puzzled child in silence,
Lonely, lost and far behind.

In imagination only,
In my single mirror see,
Clear and calm, the one reflection
Of the person that is me.

WHEN I WAS A SMALL BOY

When I was a small boy in a small school,
With endless legs
And ears that widely proclaimed a head full of
emergencies,
When I clung by bleeding fingertips
To thirty-three plus nine,
And cognitive dissonance was a hard sum,
There were only two crimes.

The first was shouting in the corridors,
The second was to be a fool,
And when the bell,
The blessed bell,
Let me fling my body home,
I thought I might, at least, one day, aspire to rule in
    hell,
But now, I never hear the bell,
And part of me
Will always be
A fool
Screaming, in some sacred corridor.

Nice

The 'Nice' sketch is a rather alarmingly raw slice of life. It involves a married couple, well practised in the art of tearing each other to pieces, battling doggedly along one of their familiar argumentative ruts. It has been our experience (I have always performed this sketch with my wife, Bridget) that it touches people and provokes response on a number of levels, especially in the case of married couples. It has no visible Christian content, but I think that's the whole point. Many married Christian couples simply cannot understand why they experience such intense and even violent conflict in a relationship which 'should' be loving and peaceful. This sketch offers no answers, but it might, like a benevolent grenade, explode some of the resistance people quite naturally feel to the idea of opening up to others who might be able to help.

'Nice' does require some acting skill and careful direction. Ideally it's performed in a pool of light. The only other things required are a suitcase which is being packed with clothes by the man as the sketch proceeds, and a single chair. Don't worry about laughs at the beginning of the sketch. They soon fade!

NICE

Man is packing. Woman is watching.

WOMAN: Why are you going?

MAN: I've had enough.

WOMAN: Enough of what?

MAN: Enough of you.

WOMAN: Enough of me what?

MAN: Enough of you asking me what I've had enough of.

WOMAN: You must have had enough of some *thing*. *(Pause)* What have you had enough of?

MAN: Well, if you must know, I've had enough of you being nice.

WOMAN: But what's ... ?

MAN: And loving, and generous, and forgiving, and ... clean.

WOMAN: What's wrong with being lov – all those things?

MAN: The thing that's wrong with being all those things is that *I'm* not. I'm unpleasant, hateful, mean, unforgiving and scruffy.

WOMAN: No, you're not.

MAN: Yes, I am.

WOMAN: No, you're not.

MAN: *(Loudly)* Yes, I am!

WOMAN: Well ... maybe you are.

MAN: No, I'm not!

WOMAN: You just said you were.

MAN: Well, I'm *allowed* to say I am. You're too *nice* to agree with me.

WOMAN: But you just said you didn't like me being nice.

MAN: No, I did not.

WOMAN: You did.

MAN: I didn't.

WOMAN: You did!

MAN: I did not. I said I'd had enough of you being nice. I have had sufficient. Thank you for supplying me with an appropriate amount of niceness. I have now had enough. I have packed all your niceness with my socks and shirts and underwear, and I am going to find someone or somewhere that will supply me with an equal amount of something else that I have not got enough of.

WOMAN: It's not fair.

MAN: Thank you for being so understanding.

WOMAN: I meant it's not fair to me.

MAN: But I just told you – I don't do fair things. *You* are fair. *I* am unfair. You are a very wonderful person, I am slightly less wonderful than a turd.

WOMAN: Don't be silly.

MAN: I am also silly.

WOMAN: You're being ridiculous.

MAN: And ridiculous.

WOMAN: What you really mean is that I never give you an excuse for doing the things you've really wanted to do since about two weeks after we got married! You'd like me to be really nasty so that you can storm out and sulk with some sympathetic stray female and moan to her about me not understanding you.

(Pause)

MAN: That's not very nice. That is not very nice at all. I have never, never, ever, ever heard you talk like that before. Never!

(Pause)

WOMAN: Look, I didn't mean *any* of that. It's not true really. I'm sorry. Please forgive me.

MAN: *(She must be joking)* Oh, yes it is! You meant every single word. And *that's* why I'm leaving. Because you think I want you to give me an excuse for doing things that you claim I've really wanted to do since about two weeks after we got married, and that I'd like you to be really nasty so that I can storm out and sulk with some sympathetic stray female and moan to her about you not understanding me. I mean – just how nasty can you get?

(She cries)

I even have to do my own packing!

WOMAN: *(Eagerly)* Let me do it for you! I'd like to...

MAN: No-o-o thanks. I'd rather do it myself.

(Pause)

Very nice of you to offer, though.

Very nice.

WOMAN: But I still don't understand what I've done wrong!

MAN: You've done nothing wrong, that's what you've done wrong. Deliberately, and with malice afore-thought, you have set out to do nothing wrong. You are an incurable, incorrigible grown-up, and I am the miserable means by which you train and strengthen the muscles of your horrible maturity. You club me with tolerant wisdom, castrate me with forgiveness, and drown me in *niceness*. You are unmercifully loving. I am getting smaller and smaller and smaller every day. I am running out of ways to bully you or make you sorry for me. I am tired of waiting for you to do something fun-damentally mean, or vicious, or disloyal, and I'm not going to wait any longer. I would like to add, though, that throughout everything, you have been unfailingly ... nice.

(Pause)

WOMAN: *(Touches him)* You won't really go. You just wanted to work yourself up so that you could say all that. It's gone now. You won't really go.

(Long pause)

MAN: You're absolutely right, of course. I won't really go. I never *do* go, do I? I expect I just – wanted to say all that.

WOMAN: Why don't we just forget about it?

(Pause)

I'll unpack for you.

(Pause)

Then I'll cook us a nice dinner.

MAN: And you promise you'll try to be just a little nastier?

WOMAN: *(She means it)* I'll do anything that makes you happy, darling. I promise.

MAN: Well, that's very – very nice of you. Very nice.

(She starts to unpack)

Stress

Stress seems to be one of the diseases of modern living, the emotional equivalent of the common cold. At its worst, though, it's a lot more than that. The whole direction of my life was changed when a severe stress reaction caused me to take early retirement (in my thirties) from work with disturbed children. It has been very satisfying to become involved in a new career, the kind of 'bits and pieces' existence I always craved, but I still experience a build-up of stress from time to time, and it is not pleasant. Fortunately I am, nowadays, aware that a tendency to become stressed is not an indication of spiritual decay, any more than David Watson's depressions were evidence of concealed problems. We are all handicapped, to one extent or another, by aspects of a temperament that we've lugged along behind us all our lives. I wouldn't for one moment wish to discount the possibility of the Holy Spirit healing or changing the negative or wounded parts of us. I know he does. I've seen it and experienced it. I would just like people to appreciate that a physical limp and an emotional handicap are not usually very different. We really do need to look after each other with lots of warmth and not much narrow-eyed insight.

'Stress' is a fairly light device for excavating this issue, and is best played mainly for laughs until the final verse, which is not very funny.

STRESS

I've just been up the doctor's. I said, 'Help me, Doctor
    Brown,'
But he said, 'You've got some tablets!' and he had this
    awful frown,
So I said, 'I've struggled up here from the other side of
    town,
Because the Downers break me up and then the Uppers
    get me down.'
I'm in a mess,
I'm under stress,
I've *tried* my best to rest without success,
I'm holding it together less and less:
I suffer stress.

Sometimes when I'm feeling very peaceful in my car,
There's some funny little clickings and I know I won't
    get far
Before the clickings turn to clunkings, and you know
    what clunkings are!
And the garage man will take a look, and frown and
    say, 'Aha!
Your car's a mess!'
It causes stress,
I've *tried* my best to rest without success,
I'm holding it together less and less:
I suffer stress.

Papers tell you food is bad, avoid the butcher's meat,
The nasty fatty stuff will clog, and knock you off your
    feet.
Everything is fatal, from meringues to shredded wheat,
If it wasn't for starvation, then I wouldn't dare to eat.

So food's a mess,
It causes stress,
I've *tried* my best to rest without success,
I'm holding it together less and less:
I suffer stress.

The world is full of terrorists who say they've been
    abused,
They're all against each other, and they're all a bit
    confused,
'Cause they murder little people, and they say when
    they're accused,
'Ah, but if your motivation's right, you have to be
    excused.'
It's just a mess,
It causes stress,
I've *tried* my best to rest without success,
I'm holding it together less and less:
I suffer stress.

There's weapons pointing east and west, they'll soon
    be flying past,
And I can't sleep for thinking that the end's approach-
    ing fast,
Every nerve is strained as I await the nuclear blast,
Still – the night they drop the bomb, I 'spose I'll get
    some sleep at last,
But what a mess,
It causes stress,
I've *tried* my best to rest without success,
I'm holding it together less and less:
I suffer stress.

I need a friend to talk to, but they're few and far
    between,
I ring them up and ask them, but they don't seem very
    keen,
I'm just as sane as they are, and I never make a scene,
They say I'm too neurotic, but *I don't know what they
    mean!*
Oh, what a mess!
It causes stress,
I've *tried* my best to rest without success,
I'm holding it together less and less:
I suffer stress.

There Won't Be Time Tonight

I've heard preachers saying that if you are walking properly with the Lord, you need never be lonely, I suppose they *could* be right. I can't help remembering how much Jesus needed his friends to stay awake and supportive at Gethsemane. I think we probably all need somebody.

We have found that this song is particularly poignant when it follows immediately after the 'Stress' poem.

This one is sung to the tune of Paul Winter's 'There Won't Be Time Tonight'.

THERE WON'T BE TIME TONIGHT

Do you ever go to bed (everyone needs a friend)
Feeling rather low (you need one)?
Do you ever lie awake, wishing the night away,
Telling yourself that soon you'll make one?

Chorus:
But there won't be time tonight
And I don't know how to try.
No one ever showed me how
Feelings are meant to fly.

Every night I go to bed, wishing I had a friend,
Everyone needs a friend, everyone needs to know
There is love.

Do you ever walk alone (tell me who made the sky?)
Feeling rather strange (where is he?)
Do you ever stand and say, maybe he touched my hand?
Maybe one day I'll say, I love him.

Chorus:
But there won't ... *etc.*

Do you ever fear your day (how can it be so long?)
Terrible fighting on (why should you?)
Hard to find a reason for moving towards the night,
Needing to hear a friend say, thank you.

Chorus:
But there won't ... *etc.*

Marvellous Me!

STORIES,
SONGS,
POEMS &
SKETCHES
by Adrian Plass

Phone Call

'Phone Call' needs very little explanation or comment. Most of us, at one time or another, have thrown ourselves into Martha-like activities in order to avoid the personal, intimate, and more deeply demanding relationship that Mary opted for. Having said that, it's worth bearing in mind that Mary probably worked just as hard as Martha when Jesus wasn't actually around.

Busyness usually looks very convincing, but unless its roots are in relationship, it's just another piece of rubbish.

Props? A small table and a telephone. The caller should be making his/her call as an afterthought just before going out.

PHONE CALL

(Picks up phone and dials a number)
Oh, Jesus – Don't come round tonight,
I'm busy at the hall,
And the chances of a chat with you
Are really rather small.
So many people need me,
And I can't deny them all,
So! It looks as if I won't be in,
If you decide to call.

Yes, Tuesday would be better,
But I think the man next door
Is looking very troubled,
And I've helped him out before.
Well – a friend in need is something
I can never quite ignore,
No – don't come round tomorrow night,
You understand, I'm sure.

(Looks at diary)
Wednesday night? That's study group,
Thursday I'm away,
On Friday I've got tickets
For the local Christian play.
Saturday's the mission,
And that'll take *all* day,
Better if we leave it now
Till Sunday night; okay?

(Pause – nearly replaces receiver. Changes mind)
Oh, Jesus? Do you love me?
Will you ever set me free?
I've built myself a prison,
I've thrown away the key.
I'm weeping in the darkness,
Yes, I'm longing now to see
The plans you have for both of us.
Please come and visit me.

Shoes

When I first met Bridget, my wife, I had only one pair of shoes. Both had large holes in the soles. I have to record that, although I would have defended my faith militantly in all sorts of awkward situations, I was too self-conscious to take Communion in an Anglican church. I couldn't bear the thought of everyone seeing the state of my footwear as I knelt at the Communion rail. Funny, fickle people we are sometimes. Anyway – that's where the idea for 'Shoes' came from. I hope it makes the point that even the most spiritual-*looking* problem can have a very practical cause, and we should never jump to conclusions. Heaven preserve us from people who think they know without asking!

All this sketch needs is a pair of telephones, one of which can be rung if possible. Ted's anger mounts slowly but perceptibly as the conversation proceeds. His final line must be heard *very* clearly.

SHOES

Richard dials a number. Ted's phone rings. He picks it up.
Richard speaks.

RICHARD: Hello! Ted?
TED: Ted here, yes. Who's that?

RICHARD: Richard here, Ted. Richard Bellbrook. Hi!

TED: Oh, yes, hello, Richard. What can I do for you? I'm a bit –

RICHARD: Ted, can I speak to you as a friend rather than as a minister?

TED: I don't know, Richard. Have a go and see.

RICHARD: Ha, ha! Very good, Ted, very good. Seriously though, I just rang on the off-chance to have a friendly chat and see how you are. See how you're getting along. Catch up on old news. Find out how the cookie's crumbling at your end of the packet. No special reason for calling. Just a friendly er ... call.

TED: Oh, right, fine.

(Pause)

RICHARD: So er ... how are you?

TED: Fine, Richard. I'm fine, thanks.

RICHARD: Good! Good! Wife okay?

TED: Fine.

RICHARD: Kids?

TED: Fine.

RICHARD: Work?

TED: Work's fine.

RICHARD: Car going all right?

TED: Bike. Had to sell the car when –

RICHARD: Bike going okay?

TED: Pedalling along nicely, thanks.

RICHARD: Any golf lately? Haven't seen you up there recently.

TED: Can't afford it, Richard, not since I lost –

RICHARD: Surviving without it, eh?

TED: Oh, fine!

RICHARD: Good, good! So overall you're...

TED: Fine, Richard. Overall, I'm just fine.

RICHARD: Good! Great! Wonderful! Marvellous! *(Pause)* Fine.

(Pause)

TED: Was that all, Richard, because I really ought to –

RICHARD: Saw you in church on Sunday, Ted.

TED: And I saw you, Richard.

RICHARD: Did you? Yes! Good! So we were er ... both there then?

TED: Looks that way, Richard, yep!

RICHARD: *(Casually)* Didn't see you up at the Communion rail though, Ted.

(Pause)

RICHARD: No sign of you kneeling up at the er ... Communion rail to take er ... communion.

(Pause)

No er ... bread or wine for you this Sunday then?

TED: That's right, Richard.

RICHARD: Nor the Sunday before that, I seem to recall.

TED: Nope!

RICHARD: Nor the Sunday before *that*, Ted.

TED: Nor the Sunday before *that*, if you must know, Richard.

RICHARD: Ted, if you're having trouble at home, I'm sure it can be sorted out. I'm more than happy to come and talk it through with you. Getting angry with the wife? Evil thoughts? Not pulling your weight in the home? Adultery? Shouting at the kids? Some little private sin? Gay?

TED: Richard, it's not –

RICHARD: There is absolutely no reason why you shouldn't kneel at that communion rail like anyone else. If you've got the time I've got the ministry, and though I say it myself, I do have a bit of a special gift when it comes to leading lost brothers and sisters through confession to repentance. Now speak up, Ted. You can't shock me. It doesn't matter what it is. Covetousness? Theft? Been dabbling in the occult?

TED: For goodness –

RICHARD: Drink? Drugs? Unbelief? Come on, Ted. What is it that's preventing you from kneeling at that rail? Cheating on tax? Sexual perversion? Spirit of criticism? What's keeping you in your seat on Sunday mornings? Greed? Spiritual pride? Idolatry?

TED: Don't be ridiculous! It's just –

RICHARD: Are we Christian brothers, Ted?

TED: Yes, but –

RICHARD: Do we trust each other?

TED: Yes, but –

RICHARD: Is there anything you'd keep from me?

TED: No, but it's –

RICHARD: So what's the problem, bro? Open up and –

TED: *(through bared teeth)* Don't call me bro!

RICHARD: Open up and share the problem, Ted! I've watched you every Sunday looking troubled when it comes to the time for communion, and I know – I just *know*, brother – that something is preventing you from standing up, walking down the centre aisle of our church, and kneeling to receive a blessing, and I feel led to counsel you now that the time has come to reveal your secret sin and find freedom!

TED: I haven't got a secret sin! It's just –

RICHARD: *(shouts)* Now is the time for courage, Ted! Gird your loins and make your mind up that you can and will unburden yourself! He will not strive for ever, and this is the acceptable day! Tell me why you cannot kneel at that communion rail!

TED: You pinhead! It's just –

RICHARD: *Tell* me why you cannot kneel at that communion rail!

TED: I don't see –

RICHARD: *Tell me why you cannot kneel at that communion rail!*

TED: It's none of your –

RICHARD: *Why can't you kneel at that communion rail?*

TED: *Because I've got holes in my shoes!!*
(*Slams down phone*)

Operation

'Operation' is an improvisation that aims to demonstrate the way in which we sometimes trample over God's expert work in the problems and difficulties of our lives. It's so easy to think that we know best, especially perhaps when it comes to timing.

OPERATION

Ideally, 'Operation' involves one adult, who plays the surgeon, and six or seven children who are nurses standing around the operating table. One more child is needed to be the prostrate 'patient'.

The scene opens with the nurses standing silently and attentively around the table as the surgeon, with intense concentration, does something to the side of the patient that is invisible to the audience. For quite a long time the only sound to be heard is an occasional curt request for a scalpel or a swab, instantly and respectfully supplied by the nurses. Children greatly enjoy the challenge of creating the tense stillness of this scene, once they understand how essential it is as a contrast to the disintegration that follows. At last, one of the nurses shows an infinitesimal hesitation in passing an instrument, but her hint of a query is instantly quashed by the surgeon, who impatiently demands the thing he's asked for and returns to his task.

From this point onwards anarchy grows, but to be really effective it must happen *very* gradually. Eventually all the nurses are arguing loudly and aggressively with the surgeon and each other, so violently in fact, that the surgeon is pushed out altogether and drifts away out of sight. The noise is hushed once more when the patient suddenly sits upright, looks at the operation site and says, 'That's not right!' The babble then continues with various improbable 'bits' being removed from the patient and thrown aside by the nurses until someone shouts, 'Hey! – he's dead!' and all exit, still arguing about what *should* have been done.

'Operation' is extremely effective as long as the need for total concentration and very gradual build-up has been understood and practised a few times.

Conforming Is Correct!

STORIES,
SONGS,
POEMS &
SKETCHES
by Adrian Plass

The Real Problem

I was a rather troubled little boy. Things confused me. I remember feeling particularly anxious about the difference between the way my father was in church every Sunday, and his behaviour at home before and after the service. The hour that we spent in the little Roman Catholic chapel at the end of the village was, all too frequently, sandwiched between much longer periods of anger and tumult. I found it difficult to understand how Dad could switch so easily into a smiling civilized mode, purely, it seemed to me, for the benefit of church acquaintances who never had to witness the scenes of domestic tension and conflict that sprang so easily from his profound insecurity. I wondered why God didn't sort it out. I knew I would have done if I'd been omnipotent.

Nowadays, with three sons under fourteen and a baby daughter who's nearly a year old, it still requires something akin to a small civil war to get everyone clean and dressed and actually moving towards the family service in our local Anglican church. Threats are hissed, small indignant faces are washed, coats are unearthed, the dog, who has tried to follow us, is taken back and incarcerated, and we are on our way at last, usually in a less than holy frame of mind. The difference between my children's experience of Sunday mornings and my own early memories is, I hope, that as a family we are much more honest with ourselves and outsiders than my father ever felt able to be. Thank God for that. Some still aren't able to be that honest.

'The Real Problem' is a simple little poem expressing this particular problem from the child's point of view. I usually adopt a childlike tone when performing it, but it isn't really essential. The point is in the words. It is usually received with a low hum of identification...

THE REAL PROBLEM

Sunday is a funny day,
It starts with lots of noise.
Mummy rushes round with socks,
And Daddy shouts, 'You boys!'

Then Mummy says, 'Now don't blame them,
You know you're just as bad,
You've only just got out of bed,
It really makes me mad!'

My mummy is a Christian,
My daddy is as well,
My mummy says, 'Oh, heavens!'
My daddy says, 'Oh, hell!'

And when we get to church at last,
It's really very strange,
'Cos Mum and Dad stop arguing,
And suddenly they change.

At church my mum and dad are friends,
They get on very well,
But no one knows they've had a row,
And I'm not gonna tell.

People often come to them,
Because they seem so nice,
And Mum and Dad are very pleased
To give them some advice.

They tell them Christian freedom
Is worth an awful lot,
But I don't know what freedom means,
If freedom's what they've got.

Daddy loves the meetings,
He's always at them all,
He's learning how to understand
The letters of St Paul.

But Mummy says, 'I'm stuck at home
To lead my Christian life,
It's just as well for blinkin' Paul
He didn't have a wife.'

I once heard my mummy say
She'd walk out of his life,
I once heard Daddy say to her
He'd picked a rotten wife.

They really love each other,
I really think they do.
I think the people in the church
Would help them – if they knew.

Legs

All my life I have bobbed and ducked and weaved to avoid losing my dignity. What a waste of time! I think I've probably learned more through my really idiotic moments than through any amount of supposed cleverness. The more we share failures and weaknesses with others, the more we seem to gain in a different kind of dignity that has nothing to do with vanity or conceit.

The 'Legs' incident, which made me feel a first class twit at the time, happened a few years ago, and resulted in me asking myself a question that has seemed increasingly important recently – as I've met so many different people in so many different types of church. When you come to the end of the article, do ask the question with me and see if it applies to you, or whether it might apply to people in your church – people who wish they'd had the courage to say how they felt right at the beginning, and fear that it may be too late now.

LEGS

Each time we go on holiday I seem to learn one lesson. That's a lot for me.

Like the time when my wife Bridget and I travelled on the coach from Victoria to Norwich. We were excited about going away for a couple of weeks but there was one small problem. My legs are quite long, and unless I sit in one of the front seats in a coach I get most uncomfortable after a short distance.

So we queued for a very long time, at a very early hour of the morning; it was tedious, but I knew it would be worth it.

Then, at the last moment, a woman nipped in ahead of us and grabbed the places we wanted. My wife displayed the kind of righteous aggression that is peculiar to people who are basically kind by nature.

'Excuse me!' she rapped. 'We've queued for these seats for a long time. My husband needs to sit here because of his legs.' The woman moved. She might have argued the point but Bridget's words had provoked a barrage of sympathetic comments from several old dears in the queue behind us.

'Poor dear ...'

'What a shame ...'

'E's got bad legs ...'

'So young ...'

''Ard for 'is wife ...'

'Yeeess ... poor soul.'

As our journey began, I sat rather stiffly and self-consciously, aware of several pairs of eyes studying my grey corduroy trousers, picturing with compassionate relish the awful putrefaction that they probably concealed. I hardly noticed the scenery.

The discussion on bad legs in general, and mine in particular, continued until we stopped halfway through our journey for refreshments at a road-side café. We were the last to get off.

As I stepped down I noticed my little support group hovering outside the café, watching with barely concealed fascination to see how the badness in my lower limbs would manifest itself when I actually walked.

I know that their expectations shouldn't have influenced me. I *know* that, but I couldn't help it. You would have been strong. I was weak. The dreadful truth is that I limped heavily and artistically from the coach to the café with Bridget laughing hysterically beside me.

Ten minutes later I felt obliged to repeat my Hunchback of Notre Dame impression on the return journey, still accompanied by my spluttering spouse. There was no doubt about the impact on my audience. They were very impressed. Not only did this poor man suffer terribly with his decaying nether regions, but he had to contend with a mentally unbalanced wife as well.

Newly inspired, they embarked on a much deeper and more wide-ranging medical discussion as the coach set off once more, a discussion that was still deep into obstetrics as we arrived at the coach station in Norwich.

I haven't got bad legs.

I don't limp.

My wife is quite sane.

What was the question I asked myself as a result of this absurd incident? It was this: How many other small, unreal worlds can be created by misunderstanding and maintained by cowardice? It can happen anywhere. In a coach, or a family, or a church.

God Says

It can be very tempting to join a group or movement because it offers types of expression and behaviour that are a pleasure to conform to. That may be right. There's nothing wrong with pleasure. But if the springs of liveliness, or liturgical soundness, or silence, or musical excellence, or whatever a particular group offers, are polluted or impure at source, then involvement can be very costly in the long run. It pays to take time and trouble checking that a superficial attraction has the right kind of substance beneath it.

'God Says' is a piece of buffoonery that makes this point in dramatic fashion. It's probably best used as a means of illustrating or emphasizing a point in the course of a presentation or talk, rather than in isolation. Points to remember are that the 'evangelist' must keep his smile on his face *all* through the piece, the crowd must *gradually* respond to his overtures, and their reaction to the shooting must be realistic. By the way, cap guns just aren't loud enough. Get hold of a starting pistol if you can.

GOD SAYS

An evangelist type (probably with American accent) jumps up onto a chair or table top and addresses the crowd loudly and aggressively. A fixed grin is plastered over his face throughout all the proceedings.

EVANGELIST: Ladies and gentlemen, I am here to tell you that church does not have to be dull and boring! Church can be exciting! Church can be fun! Church can be alive and lively! Where I come from we are never bored in church. Why are we never bored in church? Because we are in accord! Why are we in accord? Because everyone in our church agrees with what I say! I don't know why, but they do! Hallelujah?

(Crowd responds with unconvinced, muttered Hallelujahs) Where I come from we play a game in church! Yes, we do – we play a game! Brothers and sisters, I sense that you want to know what that game is! Amen?

(A stirring of interest in the crowd. A few Amens) Hallelujah! You shall know because I am going to tell you! Amen?

(Quite loud Amens from crowd) Hallelujah?

CROWD: Hallelujah!

EVANGELIST: Okay! Hallelujah! Over in this country you have a game called Simon Says. Amen?

CROWD: Amen!

EVANGELIST: Hallelujah?

CROWD: Hallelujah!

EVANGELIST: Well, in the church I come from we play a game like that, only it's not called Simon Says, it's called God Says! Amen?

CROWD: Amen! *(Really involved now)*

EVANGELIST: Hallelujah?

CROWD: Hallelujah!

EVANGELIST: Amen?

CROWD: Amen!

EVANGELIST: God Says is an easy game to play! Every time I say God says do something, you have to do it! But if God doesn't say do it, why then you don't do it! Hallelujah?

CROWD: Hallelujah!

EVANGELIST: Amen?

CROWD: Amen!

EVANGELIST: Hallelujah?

CROWD: Hallelujah!

EVANGELIST: Amen?

CROWD: Amen!

EVANGELIST: *Amen?*

CROWD: *Amen! Hallelujah!*

EVANGELIST: Shall we play the game? Amen?

CROWD: Amen!

EVANGELIST: *Hallelujah?*

CROWD: *Hallelujah! Amen!*

EVANGELIST: *(with a strong swinging rhythm)* God says put your hands on your head!

CROWD: *(Repeating his words and rhythm exactly, performing the required action as they do so. The 'evangelist' repeats the words and performs the actions with the crowd)* God says put your hands on your head!

EVANGELIST: God says put your hands on your knees!

CROWD: God says put your hands on your knees!

EVANGELIST: God says put your hands on your chest!

CROWD: *(very excited by now)* God says put your hands on your chest!

EVANGELIST: God says put your hands on your ears!

CROWD: God says put your hands on your ears!

EVANGELIST: God says put your hands in your pockets!

CROWD: God says put your hands in your pockets!

EVANGELIST: Put your hands in the air!

(One crowd member puts his hands in the air. The evangelist takes a pistol from his pocket and shoots him. He collapses, moaning and clutching his chest. The crowd gathers round him chilled and shocked)

PERSON A: You shot him! You just shot him!

EVANGELIST: Well, he shouldn't put his hands in the air when God didn't *tell* him to put his hands in the air! In this game we only do what God says!

PERSON B: But you can't shoot someone just because –

EVANGELIST: Make way there now! *(He comes through the crowd to the injured person, and speaks to him, still pointing his gun)* Get up now, you're coming with me! *(The injured one cringes back, and the crowd move as if to close in on the evangelist, but he waves them back with his gun)* GOD SAYS get up now, you're coming with me! *(The injured one hurriedly gets up and goes, followed by the evangelist, still pointing his gun)* I told you church needn't be boring! Amen? *(The crowd rumbles and boos as he leaves)*

PERSON A: *(shouting after the evangelist very loudly)* You can't shoot someone just because they don't play your game properly!

Worldliness Is Wonderful!

STORIES,
SONGS,
POEMS &
SKETCHES
by Adrian Plass

My Way

One of the games we play in the church is about lifestyle. We are very good at kidding ourselves into believing that religious activities equal Christian living. This applies just as much in new, informal churches as it does in the traditional denominations. I have encountered folk who are feverishly concerned to get 'the worship' right, but never seem to step off the circle line of Bible studies, prayer meetings and Sunday worship to expose themselves to the world that awaits Jesus. Meanwhile, their personal lifestyle remains virtually unchanged. I'm always very wary about reading the Gospels. They challenge the way I live in a gritty, practical way. Ask people I don't like to dinner? Love my enemies? Seek the kingdom of God *first*? Be honest about the way I really am? Take the lowest place? – the list is formidable. I can't manage it all, but I am convinced that one of the most dangerous fallacies around is the one that says our social and financial lives can remain safe and unchanged if we seriously intend to follow Jesus.

'My Way' is a rather absurd re-write of the famous Sinatra song (written by Paul Anka), portraying the pathetically commonplace lifestyle of someone who clearly sees himself as being quite a 'man'. Each line is ludicrously overlength for the tune, and most are best delivered in a flat, rather tuneless voice (not difficult for me). I nearly always 'sing' the song without accompaniment, unless a magician like Chris Norton is around. He amazed me at Royal Week one year by carrying my faltering tones effortlessly and faultlessly through 'My Way' without a single rehearsal.

You can get a bit fed up with performing the same things over and over again, but 'My Way' still makes *me* laugh.

MY WAY

Born, yes I was born, at the Gooseberry Bush Nursing
    Home, Farley Road in Thurston, on my birthday,
    which just happened to be a Friday.
And my mother, who has a quite extraordinary mem-
    ory for weather, tells me that it was an exception-
    ally dry day.
Apparently I was a really independent little devil even
    then, so all the people who saw me at the time say,
When I was supposed to be going to sleep I used to
    make a real old squeaky noise whenever I wanted
    my way.

School, I went like everyone else, but I didn't do very
    well there, but it wasn't my fault, it was because
    they made me sit next to a kid called Vernon Myres.
But in the end I did get one exam, I got CSE mode 3,
    grade 6, in changing tyres,
And I once made a sort of modern art thing, by acci-
    dent, in metalwork, that my mother thought was
    really good, it was a sort of ball of metal with like
    long thin wires,
But more, much more than this, I made a fruit bowl.

Refrain:
    For what is a man? What has he got? If he's not

got a reasonable income and some savings in the building society, and a membership card for the squash club, and a couple of mates to go out with once a week, with the wife's say-so, although we do almost get up to some real naughties sometimes, he's not got a lot, I've got all these now, by careful use of available resources, and I did it my way.

Girls, I've had a few, well, one, and I married her, and her name's Gloria, and she's a bit taller than me, but it doesn't matter,

'Cause I've got this really cool pair of high-heeled cowboy boots, and I make sure all her shoes are very much flatter,

I've tried to get her to walk in the gutter, while I walk up on the pavement, but it's taken a good three weeks of persuasion, drat 'er,

But after I'd pointed out that all good relationships depend on compromise, and that I'd smack her in the mouth if she didn't do what she was told, she saw it my way.

Job, I've got a job, at an insurance company, where I do rather important things connected with computers.

And every Friday at lunchtime me and some of the lads go down to the Ferret's Armpit to have more than a couple of Mackeson and orange juices,

We might, also, have a game or two of pool, if anyone's got some 50p's and there aren't any rough people in the public bar who might boot us off,

And none of us think our boss is any good but we don't say so in front of him, although we're not scared of him; he'd better not get in my way.

Refrain:

For what is a man? What has he got? If he's not got a spirit of adventure like me that leads me to choose a different south coast holiday resort every five years despite Gloria's opposition, and I once got fairly firm with a waiter who was a bit slow with the main course although I don't think he actually heard me because I said it very quietly, then he's not got a lot, I've got a small BMW, I hope to move to Surrey one day, and I'll do it my way.

(Quietly) If Gloria agrees.

Machine

'M'achine' is an improvisation illustrating very simply that the development of complex structures does not bring about change in individuals, and can in fact be dangerous in the long run to those who attempt to create and control them.

MACHINE

A mad professor type decides to build a machine. His raw materials are ten robotic human beings who are stacked carelessly in a corner, perhaps moving or stirring randomly. He brings them out two by two, and after adjusting their 'controls', places them in the position where they will perform as machine parts, probably facing each other. After establishing and testing the movements of each pair, he turns them off and brings on the next pair with whom he repeats the process.

Eventually the machine, two lines of people facing each other, is complete. The big moment has arrived. With a bang and a puff of smoke he switches on at the mains, and the machine goes into action. Delighted with his creation, he goes a little too close and drops his glasses into one end of the machine. In his attempt to recover them, he is swallowed up by the machine, and horribly 'digested' by the rows of moving parts.

Eventually, his lifeless body is passed back along the machine and thrown out at the point where he fell in. The machine is exultant. Each part can separate and roam the stage, still performing its individual movement until the music stops and all are still.

This exercise can provide a lot of fun in the planning and execution. The selection or recording of suitable machine-line music is an interesting business as well.

NB: This is not a Plass original! I took part in this exercise years ago when Diana Edwards ran the West Kent Theatre Workshop.

Party and The Dream of Being Special

PARTY

Some time ago we were faced with the problem of creating a lively party atmosphere on stage. Why a problem? Well, there were only five of us on stage, five characters who were involved in a search for some kind of truth. We solved the party problem in the end by realizing that five people talking continuously and simultaneously is the equivalent of five groups of, say, five or six folk, with only one person at a time speaking in each group. But what should we say? We decided in the end to give each character a short speech which would be repeated over and over again in a variety of tones. The speeches were as follows:

(a) Oh, it's absolutely marvellous! It's absolutely wonderful! He didn't? Oh, he did! What a scream!

(b) Completely unexpected – absolutely unanimous apparently. Didn't know I was so popular. Can't let 'em down of course.

(c) Oh, do you really think so? I'm sure you don't mean it. No one's ever said that to me before!

(d) What an extraordinary coincidence! You're not going to believe this, sweetheart, but that is *exactly* how I feel!

(e) Frankly, a car's a car to me. Just a thing to get me from A to B. Fact that it's a roller is neither here nor there.

With a bit of glass chinking and some fairly manic party-type movements, the resultant babble was extraordinary! It's a device worth remembering for any simulated crowd scene. It doesn't actually matter what the characters say, as long as they vary the tone, *don't stop talking*, and address as many people per second as possible.

The party in our stage show was supposed to be an attempt by five characters to find distraction. One by one they slowed their frenzied speech and movement until the group was just a dejected huddle. Each person then sang a verse of 'The Dream of Being Special', a song about the ways in which people seek satisfaction from the world, but ultimately find disappointment and lack of fulfilment.

Although it was presented as a song originally, I often read it as a poem. These verses concern items of 'rubbish' that people often find very difficult to dispose of.

THE DREAM OF BEING SPECIAL

And in the summer sunshine
You believed the things they told you

For it's part of being little
And the trust is right inside you
Like a ball of summer sunshine
In the middle of your body
And you think that it will never
Fade away.
But as the days go flying
You are troubled by the shadows
In the hearts and hands and faces
Of the people you had trusted
When they promised you the sunshine.
For you hear the winter now
In what they say,
And the dream of being special floats away,
And the whole damn thing looks so grey.

And how you'd love to picture
The perfection of your lover
Who would be so strong and gentle
That his love would touch your spirit
Through your mind and heart and body
And his tenderness would promise
That the joy of every day
Would be the same.
Then one day you feel frightened
When a man who seemed to like you
Puts his hands upon your shoulders
And he holds you far too tightly
And he wants to know your age
But not your name.
And the dream of being special floats away,
And the whole damn thing looks so grey.

There's a friend you meet on Fridays

He's the one who really knows you
And you tell him you're not suited
To the job that you are doing
But you drink and say don't worry
For I'm planning something different
And I've just about decided
On a scheme.
And won't it be electric
When I start my great adventure
And the talent I've been hiding
Has a chance to be discovered.
Then you see your friend is smiling
As he smiles every Friday
At your dream.
And the dream of being special floats away,
And the whole damn thing looks so grey.

And parties, they're just places
Where you lean against the doorway
Of the kitchen talking nonsense
To a girl with perfect manners
But you see her eyes are glazing
And you know she's only waiting
For the slightest little chance to
Get away.
So then you fill your glass up
As you nurse your tired passion
And remember all the failures
And you wish to God you hadn't
Overfed your fat opinions
With the food your heart was needing
Every day.
And the dream of being special floats away,

And the whole damn thing looks so grey.

And good old Michael Aspel
Would come smiling round the corner
With a big red book and people
Who would say, 'We always loved you'.
And you'd wonder why the hell they
Never told you when you needed
All the love that they could offer
What a shame.
But as he moved towards you
You would know it doesn't matter
And it's just another way to
Lose the game that you are playing
For in letters that are golden
On the big red book he'd show you
There is someone else's name.
And the dream of being special floats away,
And the whole damn thing looks so grey.

Cut-Price Christianity!

STORIES,
SONGS,
POEMS &
SKETCHES
by Adrian Plass

When I Became a Christian

I had a very definite conversion experience back in the sixties. By that I mean that a sudden vivid awareness of the reality and attractiveness of Jesus caused me to change my mind about the direction in which I wanted to go. The problem after that was that I, in common with many other converts in that period, never really appreciated that there is a difference between conversion and discipleship. Conversion is a change of mind, but discipleship involves a change of life. Perhaps the missing ingredient in the teaching of that decade was the bit about *cost*. I was interested to read somewhere that Billy Graham, when asked if he would like to have changed any aspect of his earlier teaching, replied that he would have been much more emphatic about the total demands of God on any Christian who wanted to see real power in his life. The 'happy ever after' mythology that still bedevils some areas of the church is a particularly subtle means of obscuring a truth that Jesus was absolutely open about. The Christian life is tough, and if it's to be of any real use, demands complete giving of oneself. That's why it's so important that our joy should be full, presumably.

'When I Became a Christian' started its life as a few scribbled lines in the back of a notebook. I never finished it because I didn't like it. Then in December of 1987 I was due to assist Jim Smith, the evangelist, in a 'Man Alive' meeting at the Colston Hall in Bristol. I'd been asked to contribute two or three pieces which would feed into the general theme of men taking a more dynamic and muscular role in the church. As usual I was panicking because I couldn't quite decide what my third offering should be. Then my wife Bridget discovered my unfinished verses, liked them, and felt sure that they were absolutely right for Jim's meeting. I still had little confidence in the poem, but I had, and always have had, great confidence in my wife's judgement in these matters. I finished the thing off, took it to Bristol with me, and used it at the Colston Hall. Bridget was right.

It's about cost, and if you read it in public, it's worth taking your time. The gaps and pauses are probably more eloquent than the words.

WHEN I BECAME A CHRISTIAN

When I became a Christian I said, Lord, now fill me in,
Tell me what I'll suffer in this world of shame and sin.
He said, Your body may be killed, and left to rot and
    stink,
Do you still want to follow me? I said, Amen – I think.
I think Amen, Amen I think, I think I say Amen,
I'm not completely sure, can you just run through that
    again?
You say my body may be killed and left to rot and
    stink,
Well, yes, that sounds terrific, Lord, I say Amen – I
    think.

But, Lord, there must be other ways to follow you, I
    said,
I really would prefer to end up dying in my bed.
Well, yes, he said, you could put up with sneers and
    scorn and spit,

308

Do you still want to follow me? I said, Amen! – a bit.
A bit Amen, Amen a bit, a bit I say Amen,
I'm not entirely sure, can we just run through that
again?
You say I could put up with sneers and also scorn and
spit,
Well, yes, I've made my mind up, and I say, Amen! – a
bit.

Well I sat back and thought a while, then tried a dif-
ferent ploy,
Now, Lord, I said, the Good Book says that Christians
live in joy.
That's true, he said, you need the joy to bear the pain
and sorrow,
So do you want to follow me, I said, Amen! – tomorrow.
Tomorrow, Lord, I'll say it then, that's when I'll say
Amen,
I need to get it clear, can I just run through that again?
You say that I will need the joy, to bear the pain and
sorrow,
Well, yes, I think I've got it straight, I'll say,
Amen – tomorrow.

He said, Look, I'm not asking you to spend an hour
with me,
A quick salvation sandwich and a cup of sanctity,
The cost is you, not half of you, but every single bit,
Now tell me, will you follow me? I said, Amen! – I quit.
I'm very sorry, Lord, I said, I'd like to follow you,
But I don't think religion is a manly thing to do.
He said, Forget religion then, and think about my Son,
And tell me if you're man enough to do what he has
done.

Are you man enough to see the need, and man enough
  to go,
Man enough to care for those whom no one wants to
  know,
Man enough to say the thing that people hate to hear,
To battle through Gethsemane in loneliness and fear.
And listen! Are you man enough to stand it at the end,
The moment of betrayal by the kisses of a friend,
Are you man enough to hold your tongue, and man
  enough to cry,
When nails break your body – are you man enough to
  die?
Man enough to take the pain, and wear it like a crown,
Man enough to love the world and turn it upside down,
Are you man enough to follow me, I ask you once
  again?
I said, Oh, Lord, I'm frightened, but I also said Amen.
Amen, Amen, Amen, Amen; Amen, Amen, Amen,
I said, O Lord, I'm frightened, but I also said, Amen.

Books

One Christmas I was asked by one of my favourite local churches, Frenchgate Christian Centre in Eastbourne, to put together an 'Entertainment with a message' for the Sunday before Christmas day. It ended up as a collection of sketches and verse linked by a narrator who was searching for Jesus. 'Books' is an extract from that presentation, the main body of which can be used separately if the name of the preacher/pastor/vicar is localized. I've left it in context here to show how it fitted into the general theme, and also to bring eternal fame to Geoff Booker, a good friend of mine who at that time worked for Kingsway Publications (he says), and used to attend the church where 'Books' was first performed. In fact, as you can tell from the extract, he was supposed to be the one who actually recited the lines, but a rather nasty accident forced him to drop out, so I had to do it. 'Ecclestone' is Ben Ecclestone, an elder at Frenchgate. He has no connection with Kingsway, but plenty of other problems. If you want to use the main section, just substitute your own church leader's name for Ben's.

For the piece to be effective you need *lots* of books, probably forty or fifty, on a table within easy reach of the performer. Careful rehearsal and preparation pay dividends with 'Books'.

The point of this piece is not that I believe all Christian paperbacks to be bad or useless. That would be a very strange attitude for a writer of Christian books to adopt. Rather, it is that there are probably too many books, and too much of a tendency on the part of readers to seek final solutions in the printed word. The best Christian books are signposts pointing towards Jesus.

BOOKS

NARRATOR: Excuse me, Mr Booker, sir,
    I'm told – despite your looks –
    You're really rather clever,
    And you're something big in books.
    They say you work for Kingsway.
    Is that right? Do you agree?
GEOFF: Well, yes, except that I would say,
    That Kingsway works for me.
NARRATOR: But listen, Mr Booker,
    Could you put us on the track
    Of Jesus? Have you seen him?
    Is he there in paperback?
GEOFF: *(holds up books continually as he speaks)*
    Everything's in paperback!
    All you need to know,
    Little gems of cosmic truth,
    At fifty bob a throw.
    We cover every subject,
    From repentance to the pill,
    If no one's done a book on it,
    We'll find a man who will.
    The formula's a piece of cake,
    It always seems to work:
    'I'm good and happy nowadays,
    I used to be a berk.'
    This one says 'seek unity,

For heart to heart should speak',
And this one deals with other faiths,
And why they're up the creek.
And if you fear that Ecclestone*
Is stringing you along,
Well, this one claims he could be right,
And these five prove he's wrong.
Here's a book that frowns on drink,
But tells you how to search,
For pubs that don't get visited
By people from the church.
Books for Sunday, books for Monday,
Books from north and south,
Books that tell you when to speak
And when to shut your mouth.
Books that don't say very much,
(Holds up very thick book)
And books that say a lot,
(Holds up very thin book)
Books on why the church is dead,
And books on why it's not.
Books on love and books on praise,
And lots of books on prayer,
Books on how to eat and sleep
And breathe, and wash your hair.
Books on life and death and piles
And drains and constipation,
One on how to tell yourself
You don't like fornication.
Books on washing Christian shirts,
And treating Christian 'flu',

---

*Substitute local pastor's name.

On how to shut the Christian door,
And flush the Christian loo.
Books on sinners, books on saints,
Con-men, cads and crooks,
Books on everything in sight,
There's even books on books.
There's books and books and books and books,
And books and books and books,
And books and books and books and books
And books and books and books.
Jesus? Well, he's not in stock,
I'll get him – well, I'll try.
But is he fact or fiction?
And who's he published by?
I've got a book *about him*,
Or a pamphlet, or a tract,
He may be here for all I know,
There's one box not unpacked.
NARRATOR: No thank you, Mr Booker, sir,
Despite your verbal sprint,
I don't believe I'll find him here,
Perhaps he's out of print.

Nathan Rap

One of the most dramatic pieces of rubbish-clearing in the Old Testament section of the Bible must be Nathan the prophet's confrontation with King David after the Bathsheba and Uriah incident. David, hitherto a 'man after God's own heart', summoned the beautiful Bathsheba to his palace one night, slept with her, and sent her home in the morning. She became pregnant. Having failed to cover up his adulterous crime by devious means, he arranged for Bathsheba's husband, Uriah, an army captain, to be killed on the field of battle. He then brought the widow back to his palace and married her himself. How he ever thought he would escape retribution for these gross infringements of God's law is difficult to say, except that in my own life, I know how capable I am of shutting out the voice of conscience when I want something badly enough.

David did get his comeuppance. Nathan the prophet told the king a little story about a poor man who lost the only thing he had. David didn't catch on at all – not until Nathan explained. Then, he was devastated.

'Nathan Rap' is the story in verse of that encounter between Nathan and David. It's actually part of a one-hour dramatic presentation of the David and Bathsheba story, involving narration and music, written by myself and James Hammond. This section stands perfectly well on its own, but it's as well to be familiar with the story as a whole if you decide to use it. David's story begins in the sixteenth chapter of the first book

of Samuel, and finishes with his death in the second chapter of
the first book of Kings. An amazingly detailed account of an
extraordinary life.

NATHAN RAP

It was evening in the palace when the prophet came by,
There was trouble in his manner, there was thunder in
    his eye,
He was still for a moment, he was framed in the door,
And the king said, 'Nathan!... What are you here for?'
The prophet said, 'David, I've a tale to tell,'
So the king sat and listened as the darkness fell,
While the hard-eyed prophet took a seat and began,
The story of a merciless and evil man.

'This man,' said Nathan, 'had a mountain of gold,
Sheep by the thousand he bought and sold,
He never said, 'Can I afford it or not?'
What this man wanted, this man got!
And one thing he wanted, and he wanted real bad,
Was the only living thing that a poor man had,
And he knew that it was wrong, but he took it just the
    same.'
'I'll kill him!' said the king, 'Just tell me his name!'

'It was a lamb,' said the prophet, 'just a little baby
    lamb,
But he saw it and he took it and he didn't give a damn,
And he knew that it was special, and he knew it was
    a friend,
And he knew about the sadness that would never, never
    end,

316

And that same man began to plan a far more evil thing.'
Then David rose and cried aloud, 'He'll reckon with
    the king!'
'So do you think,' said Nathan, 'we should stop his
    little game?'
'I'll smash him!' shouted David, 'tell me his name!'

'Be careful,' said the prophet, 'don't go overboard,'
For David's eyes were shining like the blade of a sword,
'Perhaps you should be merciful, perhaps you should try
To understand the man before you say he must die.'
But David said, 'I understand that wrong is always
    wrong,
I am the king, I must defend the weak against the strong.'
Then Nathan questioned softly, 'So this man must take
    the blame?'
And the king was screaming, 'Nathan! Will you tell
    me his name?'

Then a silence fell upon them like the silence of a tomb,
The prophet nodded slowly as he moved across the
    room,
And, strangely, as he came he seemed more awesome
    and more wise,
And when he looked at David there was sadness in his
    eyes.
But David's anger burned in him, he drew his sword
    and said,
'I swear, before the dawn has come, that sinner will
    be dead!
No more delay, no mercy talk, give me his name!' he
    cried,
Then Nathan said, 'It's you, it's you!' and the king just
    died.

Away in a Gutter and A Father Knows No Sadness

I've had the same problems with my reaction to starvation in the Third World as most people, I imagine. I find it very difficult to unjumble all the thoughts and feelings that are provoked by pictures of dying children and despairing communities. 'So what?' say some, 'your terrible unjumbling problems are of very little interest to kids who'll be dead next week unless someone does something. Get your wallet out!'

Of course that's true; how can it not be? And yet I can't help feeling that, when it comes to Christians, unless their desire to give arises from a real understanding of and identification with the suffering Christ, then psychological and spiritual gears have a tendency to crunch horribly. The twenty-fifth chapter of Matthew's gospel explains it, and Mother Teresa's words, 'He has no hands but our hands', express it perfectly. So did her life.

'Away in a Gutter' and 'A Father Knows No Sadness' are trying to highlight the two essential facts that Jesus is in the dying child, and that if we truly love one, we will soon learn to love the other.

'Away in a Gutter' should be sung just as 'Away in a Manger' is sung, preferably by a single child or small group of

children. 'A Father Knows No Sadness' fits well to the tune of
'O Jesus, I Have Promised', and can simply be sung as a hymn.

AWAY IN A GUTTER

Away in a gutter,
No food and no bed,
The little Lord Jesus
Hangs down his sweet head.
The stars in the bright sky
Look down and they say,
'The little Lord Jesus
Is wasting away.'

We love you Lord Jesus,
We hope you survive.
We'll see you tomorrow
If you're still alive.
You won't live for long now
With no tender care.
You're best off in heaven,
We'll see you up there.

The darkness is lifting,
The baby awakes,
But little Lord Jesus,
No movement he makes.
No flesh on his body,
No light in his eye,
The little Lord Jesus
Is going to die.

A FATHER KNOWS NO SADNESS

A father knows no sadness,
No deeper-searching pain,
Than children who have taken,
But will not give again.
What profit from his loving,
If love is never shared,
What insult to his giving,
If nothing can be spared?

They wait for our remembrance,
The ones who live in need,
The ones our father trusts us
To shelter and to feed.
And if you truly love him,
Then they are precious too,
And if they are a burden,
That burden is for you.

And one day when he asks us,
To say what we have done,
Our answers will go flying
Towards the setting sun.
And how we shall remember
The truth that we were told,
As every word that leaves us
Is burned, or turned to gold.

Snowdon

As a newly converted teenager I experienced quite deep feelings of hostility towards the man who wrote the book of James in the New Testament. Fancy spoiling all that comfortable 'justified by faith' stuff by talking about works! Why on earth did the man have to go defining religion as 'staying untainted by the world and helping widows and orphans'? I fancied I could see James in my mind's eye. A sort of no-nonsense sports-master type who thought poetry was cissy and words were things to be hurled around like sports equipment. I wanted to stay enjoyably embroiled in the theory, not complicate things by getting involved in the practice.

It's so easy to get locked into an endless round of (quite laudable) religious exercises, and never actually do anything. Nowadays James is one of my favourite books, and I think the writer has a lot more poetry in him than I ever realized.

'Snowdon' is an adaptation of 'Letter to William', a story from my book *The Final Boundary*. I suppose it's really about facing the true cost of following Jesus. Quite a challenge.

The directions that I've included are only suggestions of course, but it is important that the lights fade to nothing at the end of Angerage's final speech and that the two characters are frozen until all is blacked out.

SNOWDON

A man is working at a desk. There is nothing special about him. He looks pleasant enough. An empty chair awaits visitors on the other side of the desk. There is a knock on the door. The man, whose name is Bill Angerage, looks up.

ANGERAGE: *(Brightly)* Come in, just push!

VAUGHN: *(Enters nervously, holding a piece of paper)* Mister er ... Angerage?

ANGERAGE: *(Gets up and comes across to greet him)* Bill Angerage. Call me Bill. You must be Mister Vaughn. Right?

VAUGHN: Yes, that's right, I er ... phoned earlier to make an er ... appointment.

ANGERAGE: *(Gestures towards the spare chair and resumes his own seat)* Take a seat and relax, Mister Vaughn. What's your first name?

VAUGHN: Er ... Timothy – Tim.

ANGERAGE: Okay, Tim. Fire away! What can we help you with?

VAUGHN: *(Unfolds his piece of paper as he speaks)* Well, you see – I just happened to see your er ... your er...

ANGERAGE: *(Smiles and nods)* Our announcement?

VAUGHN: Yes, your announcement. I just happened to see your announcement in the paper, and – well at first I thought it was a joke –

ANGERAGE: No joke, Tim.

VAUGHN: Yes-no-well, that's what I wasn't sure about. I kept reading it over and over again, and the more I read it, the more I thought I'd better make sure. It seemed a bit ... *(He reads from the piece of paper carefully)* 'United Kingdom Christian Recruitment Centre. We are now the *sole (emphasises "sole")* agents for salvation et al in England, Wales, Scotland and Northern Ireland. Visitors warmly welcomed. Please ring Freephone ZAP for quick appointments. Caution: previous arrangements may *not* be valid. We will advise with pleasure.' *(Looks up worriedly)*

ANGERAGE: And that we will, Tim. And more than happy to do so. *(Beams)*

VAUGHN: Thank you. The thing is Mister Ang –

ANGERAGE: Bill!

VAUGHN: The thing is, er ... Bill, that I really *do* want to be a Christian –

ANGERAGE: *(Interrupts, leaping to his feet)* Tim, that's great! *(Comes round the desk and almost hugs Tim in his delight. His pleasure is totally genuine)* That is really wonderful news! I can't tell you how it makes me feel to hear those words. Thank you so much for letting me be the one to hear them. Let me shake your hand! *(He pumps his hand)*

VAUGHN: *(Somewhat overwhelmed)* Thanks Mist – Bill, I'm glad you're pleased – actually, I er ... sort of thought I already was one. I go to a church that's quite lively, and I've made a commitment and I go to a Bible study group, and I pray – a bit, and we have the gifts and outreach and – and er ... all that, so *(looks at paper again)* I don't quite see...

ANGERAGE: *(Nodding seriously, moves back to his chair)* Tim, let's get down to business. As you've probably gathered from reading this little announcement of ours in the paper, things have changed a lot – radically I might say. The whole caboodle of prayer, Bible study, church services, et cetera has been scrapped. *(Tim is about to interrupt)* Direct orders from HQ, Tim.

VAUGHN: You mean ...? *(Points ceiling-wards)*

ANGERAGE: *(Nods solemnly)* Direct orders, Tim. All that stuff goes out the window. No need any more for discussions about salvation by faith, or about who's in or who's out. The whole thing's been completely redesigned. You can still get *(counts them off on one hand)* total forgiveness, eternal life, love, joy, and peace, the whole package as before, but the terms are different – very different.

VAUGHN: But, Mister Angerage –

ANGERAGE: Call me Bill, Tim, there's a good chap.

VAUGHN: Bill, all those things you said don't matter any more – if we don't have those – I mean, what's left? What do we have to do?

ANGERAGE: Aah, well! Now we come to it, Tim my friend. What indeed? Listen – all you have to do now is climb Snowdon three times every week! *(Leans back)*
(Long pause)

VAUGHN: *(Stunned)* Snowdon...

ANGERAGE: Yep!

VAUGHN: Three times...

ANGERAGE: Every week! That's the long and short and the top and the bottom of it, Tim my friend.

VAUGHN: But ... why?

ANGERAGE: Ours not to reason why, mate. If HQ says that's the way it's to be done, then that's the way it's to be done. Faith! That's what you need. The instructions are very simple. Snowdon – three times a week.

VAUGHN: And there's no other way to get forgiveness and peace and – all the rest?

ANGERAGE: *(Slowly)* No other way, my friend. Worth it though – isn't it?

VAUGHN: Oh, yes – yes, of course. *(Pauses, then bursts out)* But what happens about my job, Bill? I work a hundred miles away from Snowdon. I mean, I wouldn't be able to carry on with what I'm doing now, would I? Good heavens … it must take a day to climb right up Snowdon and down again, so that means three days *plus* the travelling. I'd hardly have time to do anything, let alone get a decent job of any sort. I wouldn't have any money. I wouldn't –

ANGERAGE: Any savings, Tim?

VAUGHN: I've got a few thousand in the building society, yes, but I didn't want to touch that until … *(A fresh thought)* What about friends? How do I keep up with my friends? I'll hardly ever see them – they'll think I've gone mad. They'll think … Look Bill – Mister Angerage *(Angerage raises a finger)* – Bill, this doesn't seem right. All you have to do in the church I'm in is make a personal commitment and get baptized by immersion. You don't have to go anywhere or do anything much…

ANGERAGE: *(Kindly)* Tim, don't you think the travelling, or even living down in Wales itself might be worth it if you get eternal life and happiness in return? After all, you've come to see me today, so it must mean something to you. You've got this far, mate.

VAUGHN: *(Ponders)* Do some people come to see you and then decide not to … go ahead then?

325

ANGERAGE: *(Sighs deeply)* The vast majority, I'm sad to say. Some of 'em try to compromise, despite the fact that I always make it quite clear that the three climbs are an absolute base-line minimum.

VAUGHN: *(Interested despite himself)* How do they compromise then?

ANGERAGE: Well, there's one church north of here for instance. The minister came down to see me – he'd seen that announcement just like you – said he agreed with everything I told him, went off happily back home and wrote me a letter a few weeks later to say he'd discussed the whole thing with the church council and they'd come up with an *inspired* idea. They hired a carpenter to construct a four-foot high model of Snowdon with two steps going up one side, and two going down the other. They've built it into the service. It comes just between the third hymn and the sermon.

VAUGHN: *(Hopefully)* And that doesn't count?

ANGERAGE: It's not climbing Snowdon three times a week. *(There is a pause. Vaughn is about to say something but changes his mind. He takes a Biro and a piece of paper from his pocket and starts jotting something. Angerage waits patiently. At last Vaughn looks up with hopeful enthusiasm)*

VAUGHN: Bill, listen! I've just been thinking. There must be other jobs that need doing besides the actual climbing. Supposing I adapted all the choruses we sing at the moment so that they fit the new way of things? *(He is suddenly inspired)* We could call it the Snowdon Songbook!

(Bill slowly shakes his head, but Vaughn is quite carried away now)

Look, I've just been trying one or two out. Er ... this one for instance. 'Hallelujah I'm a Christian' – you know the one I mean. This is what it sounds like when it's changed. Listen – listen! *(He sings, refer-ring to his notes sometimes)*

Hallelujah, I'm a climber,
I climb all day,
I climb up Snowdon,
Climb all the way,
Hallelujah, I'm a climber,
I climb all day.

ANGERAGE: *(Gently)* Tim, I don't think –
VAUGHN: Just a minute! Just a minute! What d'you think about this one? Used to be 'Marching to Zion'. Listen! *(Sings again – rather feverishly)*

We're marching to Snowdon,
Beautiful, beautiful Snowdon,
We're marching upward to Snowdon,
The beautiful mountain of God.

And what about this one ...

What a friend we have in Snowdon,
All our climbing gear we wear,
What a –

ANGERAGE: *(Interrupts with great authority)* No, Tim! It's no good simply singing about it. You've got to *do* it! You've *got* to climb Snowdon three times every week! *(Stands and takes a pace or two before speaking again)* Why, I could take you to a town only a few miles from here where they've set up Snowdon counselling services, Snowdon discussion groups, and courses in the real meaning of climbing. But none of them actually do it! One of our chaps who comes from that same town, and pops up from Wales very occasionally, isn't allowed into any of those groups because he's 'in error' with his simplistic approach to Snowdon. No, Tim, if you want to write some songs to keep you going while you're on the slopes, then that's fine – good idea in fact. But not instead of! Won't wash with HQ you see.

VAUGHN: *(Pathetically)* I don't even like travelling much.

ANGERAGE: Well, it's up –

VAUGHN: *(Slapping the table in triumph)* I'm not fit! I won't get up there – not even once! It's not fair! What about that?

ANGERAGE: *(He's heard it all before)* All you've got to do is turn up and climb as far as you can; and we'll make sure you get to the top from there, even if you have to be carried to the nearest mountain railway stop. Don't worry! Young chap like you, you'll be fit as a fiddle in no time. Wouldn't surprise me if you were nearly running up inside a fortnight.

VAUGHN: Do I have to decide now, Bill? I'm not quite...

ANGERAGE: Look, Tim, you go off home, have a good think about it and let me know what you decide. If you want to go ahead we'll give you a hand with the practical side. Okay?

VAUGHN: *(Gets up. Moves slowly towards the door. Angerage follows him)* All right, Bill, I'll go home and – and think about it.

ANGERAGE: *(Shakes Vaughn's hand and opens the door)* Good to meet you, Tim. I'm sure you'll make the right decision.

VAUGHN: *(Bursting out just as he is about to exit)* I just don't see what was so wrong with the old way anyway! The people in my church never did anyone any harm! Why do you want to go and make it all much harder?

ANGERAGE: You really haven't understood at all, have you Tim? We haven't made it harder – we've made it much much easier...

Fade down to darkness

Hope Is Hopeless!

STORIES,
SONGS,
POEMS &
SKETCHES
by Adrian Plass

Hope Poems

The following four short poems are all, in their own way, expressions of hope or optimism. 'Daffodils' is simply a tribute to one of the most beautiful things I know. I'm crazy about flowers. My wife quite often buys me a bunch of cut blooms to put on my desk while I write. What's that got to do with God? 'Whatsoever is lovely ...' Every now and then you encounter Christians who are wary about 'undue appreciation' of natural things. For me, a walk over the Downs in the middle of an autumn sunset says more about a personal loving God than most sermons.

'Gatwick Airport' is the result of simply sitting in the middle of passenger bustle, enjoying the complexity and variety of what's going on around me. I love Gatwick. A restless village. In the middle of it all there's a chapel for anybody to use. I'm sure it *is* used, but I've never seen anyone else in there. It seems so right, though, that there is a still heart in the centre of such a busy place.

'Winter Walk': I've so enjoyed watching my children as they discover wonderful things for the first time. One of the things I often ask God to renew in me is that capacity for wonder and enjoyment of simple pleasures, especially the free ones. Perhaps I'll be fitted with fresh, non-rust enjoyment apparatus when I get to heaven. I hope so.

'I Watch' reflects an important dawn in my life, at a time when I had thought the night was going to be very long indeed.

It came as rather a shock to realize that God must be at *least*
as nice as my mother...

DAFFODILS

Daffodils are not flowers.
They are natural neon from the dark earth,
Precious metal grown impatient,
Beaten, shaped, and dipped in pools
Of ancient, sunken light.
Folded, packed, and parachuted through,
To stand and dumbly trumpet out
The twice triumphant sun.

GATWICK AIRPORT

Sad, robotic, angel voices
Softly, sweetly speaking
To a thousand restless souls
Of gateways and departures
To a hundred different lands,
That may flow with milk and honey
Or lay heavy on the spirit
Like the old Egyptian sands.

WINTER WALK

I wish I was my son again,
The first in all the world to know
The cornflake crunch of frosted grass

Beside the polar paving stones,
Beneath the drip of liquid light
From watercolour winter suns.

I WATCH

I watch,
Frightened,
Helpless
But secretly willing,
As my foot rises, moving forward with my weight,
And I realize
That at last
I am going to walk.

Shades of Blue

I was once introduced at a meeting as 'Adrian Plass, who some of us may feel asks more questions than he provides answers for'. A doubtful recommendation on the face of it, but thinking the comment over afterwards I felt more relieved than otherwise. Anyone who's been involved in public Christian work knows how easy it is to paper over the cracks in one's own understanding of faith and present a shiny and possibly intimidating 'wonderfulness' to folk who are often all too ready to sink into a slough of spiritual inferiority. You have to be careful, though, if you do try to avoid the shiny path of cubed spirituality. The truth is not very popular in some parts of the church. But then that's always been the case, hasn't it?

The other thing that comforted me about that introductory comment was the reflection that Jesus prefaced many of his remarks with a question rather than a statement. 'What think ye ...?'

'Shades of Blue' is a whimsical attempt to show how God is quietly present even in the half-light of my temperament. Four out of the five verses are questions, and the fifth is not exactly 'call to the front' material, but it is true, and it reflects the awareness I have nowadays that he is always there, gently caring.

SHADES OF BLUE

Does winter end in seaside towns
When councils paint anew
The railings on the promenade
In hopeful shades of blue?

And if the tide loved Brighton beach
Would God come down and say
With gentle hands upon the surf
'You need not turn today?'

Will massive Church of England bells
Have faith enough to ring
And overcome their weariness
When they believe in Spring?

Are there machines for measuring
The power of my prayers
And anyway, and anyway,
And anyway, who cares?

I think you care, but gently,
I think, because you do,
The colour of my sadness
Is a hopeful shade of blue.

I Want to Be with You

The phrase 'praise and worship' has jelled in my conscious-ness like 'Morecambe and Wise', or 'Fish and Chips'. After you've used and heard the same phrase thousands of times it becomes oddly meaningless. I don't mean that I don't like doing it. I do. I especially like silent or musically accompanied meditative praise and worship. I like singing choruses, as long as I don't get told off about what I'm doing with my face or my feet. I like singing hymns and meaning them. I sometimes like speaking 'praise and worship' to God, if the words come naturally. That's the problem for me, and it applies to most religious/spiritual activities. How do you stay natural? What is a genuine statement to God going to sound like? How do I stop things like 'praise-and-worship' coagulating into meaningless lumps of activity?

This issue crystallized for me in 1986, when, as a member of CAFE, the Christian Arts Fellowship in Eastbourne, I was involved in the writing of a Christian revue for production in one of the local theatres. We needed a final song – something that completely avoided religious clichés, but was nevertheless a strong and honest statement of faith and hope. I dug into myself as far as I dared, and produced 'I Want to Be with You', a mixture of doubt, entreaty, fear and hope. It really was what I felt I would want to say to God when the crunch came. The bottom line was 'HELP!'

The verses were spoken over a pre-recorded musical

backing, the chorus ('I want to be with you' repeated eight times) was sung. One day I'd love to do this song with a large choir or congregation joining in with the chorus.

There's no harm in finding out what your spiritual bottom line is and putting it into words. Try it!

I Want to Be with You

Words and music: Adrian Plass

CHORUS

I want to be__ with you,__
I want to be__ with you,__
I want to be__ with you,__ I want to be__ with you.__
I want to be__ with you,__ I want to be__ with you,__
I want to be__ with you,__ I want to be__ with you,
I want to be__ with you.__

I WANT TO BE WITH YOU

When the steamer has sailed
And my journey has failed,
When the switches are on
But the power has gone,
When I open my eyes
But the sun doesn't rise,
When it's dark on the screen
Where the picture has been,
When there's nobody there
To pretend that they care,
When it comes to the end
And I long for a friend,
When I wish that I knew
What the hell I should do
I want to be with you.

I want to be with you. (x 8)

When the people I've known
Have gone and left me alone,
When the things that I said
Are sounding empty and dead,
When I reach for the phone
But it's dead as a stone,
When my talk about God
Is feeling foolish and odd,
When the thoughts in my mind
Have left my feelings behind,
When the skin on my hand
Becomes as dry as the sand,
When the pain in my heart
Begins to tear me apart,

Will I remember what's true?
I hope I know what to do,
I want to be with you.

I want to be with you. (x 8)

When the silence has come
And the singers are dumb,
When we stand in the light
And it's pointless to fight,
When I see what they find
In the back of my mind,
When there's no one to blame
For the sin and the shame,
When I wait for the word
To let me fly like a bird,
But I fear in my heart
I wouldn't know how to start,
When the tears in my eyes
Are blurring over the skies,
When I suddenly claim
To remember your name,
When I see that it's you
Coming out of the blue,
I want to be with you.

I want to be with you. (x 8)

Letter to Lucifer

etter to Lucifer' is a literary device, not a spiritual one. It's important to make that point because, although I think that letters to God are an excellent idea, I'm very much less sure about the advisability of writing to the devil. I don't want a reply. This then is *what* I would write, *if* I wrote, not an actual attempt to communicate with the devil.

I conclude this book with it because it sums up so much that I've wanted and tried to say. Things about deception and confusion and, especially, things about Jesus, who became a piece of human rubbish so that we could become clean. May we all understand and appreciate that a little more each day.

LETTER TO LUCIFER

Dear Lucifer,

I've been out walking in the rain today. One of those mellow spring showers, falling in big, splashy, warm drops – like the tears that Alice shed when she grew too tall for Wonderland – and I thought of you.

Now, I'm well aware that when this letter was put into your hands, the first thing you did was to flick through the pages until you came to my signature at the end. Then, I should imagine, you slapped the paper, threw your head back and laughed like a drain.

What a scream! That clown Plass attempting some feeble communication with His Infernal Majesty. Plass, who – over the last twenty years or so – has provided such a rich and consistent source of entertainment for you and yours.

Plass, who has become almost institutionalized into a devils' training ground, where even the most unskilled, love-besmirched little novice could hardly do him less good than he does himself. No doubt you've called a few of the lads over to listen as you read out what is bound to be real laugh-a-minute stuff. Well, gather round by all means, chaps. You will have a few laughs, but – there's something else as well.

First of all, and I'm sure you remember it well, there was my 'conversion' back in the sixties. You lot found the word 'conversion' a real rib-tickler back in those days, didn't you? Cheap salvation, cut-price Christianity, lots of happy-ever-after talk, and a minefield of guilt and failure to stumble through afterwards. Oh, it was real enough to start with. God called me that day as surely as if he'd blown a trumpet, clear and sweet, from the sky. (Did you read *that* bit out loud, Lucifer?) But after that you took over and – yes, you really screwed me up. You made sure that no one talked to me about cost and depth and maturity, and, above all, you used every device you knew to hide from me the fact (and it is a fact, Lucifer) that God is very *nice*, and he *likes* me. You never minded me using words like 'marvellous' and 'omnipotent', or phrases like 'everlasting love', and 'Holy Redeemer'. They just increased my inadequacy – made me feel even more small and wretched. You did a good job, let's face it. In the end I saw God as a cross between a headmaster and a bank manager, and my miserable self as a wicked little schoolboy with a horrendous overdraft.

Yes, all right, have a good laugh. Cackle away, fellers! I can see it from your point of view. Good piece of work; a really solid platform for the building of a lifetime of confusion and pretence. Because I went on to do what so many others do, didn't I? I tried to copy the people and the behaviour that I saw around me. Hands in the air, leaping about, impassioned singing, shouts of 'Hallelujah!' and 'Praise the Lord!' I was like a big half-witted puppet, and there's not much doubt about who was pulling the strings either, is there, Lucifer? You really worked me! Up and down and round and round and to and fro I went.

But I'm sure the time you liked best, the bit of my day that you really licked your lips over, was that moment when I finally got home at night, and I was on my own. Suddenly, as I walked through my own front door – your timing was always perfect – you would just let go of the strings, and everything in me would crumple and collapse. All my words, my spiritual effusions, my confident references to 'the Lord', became nothing but lines in a performance, embarrassing in their hollowness. I'll bet I was your own special little nightly soap opera – something to put your feet up and enjoy without effort.

Did you get a little round of applause when you read out that last bit, Lucifer? You deserve it. You did well.

Of course, *I* couldn't understand it at all. Why didn't God come home with me at night? Why did I only believe in him when I was surrounded by other Christians? Why, Lucifer, I hardly believed in my *own* existence, let alone God's! I felt like a hologram, a projection of the feelings and attitudes and reactions of others. No real substance of my own, nothing to hang on to and feel safe. It was a nightmare for me and a triumph for you. Once again you had succeeded in performing one of the neatest tricks of all – taking a person who had 'become a Christian' and making him more abjectly miserable than before. And the supreme joke of it all – from your point of view that is – was that if I blamed anyone, it wasn't you, it was God. Everything was God's fault! He was a nasty, harsh, narrow moralist who had little time to waste on weaklings and sinners like me.

It took me twenty years to see through the lies you told me then. Twenty years of spiritual switch-back riding. Up to the peaks, and down – way down – to the troughs. Brittle ecstasy or clogging despair, but mostly despair. And yet – something else was happening as well.

Far be it from me to offer you advice, Lucifer, but if I were you I'd dismiss that little audience of yours at this point. The next bit won't be too good for morale.

You see, the something else was Jesus. Go on, read that name out good and loud. Jesus! Shout it so loud that it trumpets through hell like an obscenity in a convent. I'm talking, of course, about the *real* Jesus, not the Weary Willie nor the vindictive hardcase that your publicity department has had so much success with.

He stayed with me through all those years. Granted, he was often little more than the faintest of nightlights in the darkness, but the point is, Lucifer, he was there; greater than the foolishness of church institutions; greater than my sins and silliness; greater than any attempt to leave him behind, and in the end, Lucifer, greater – much greater – than you. I've been reading about him in the Gospels and seeing him properly for the first time.

For years I was one of the millions who think they've read and understood about that incredible three-year ministry, but I hadn't, not really – you saw to that. In fact, you've managed to divert huge numbers of present-day Christians away from the first four books of the New Testament, haven't you? You've got them combing minutely through all sorts of other books, squeezing individual verses, or even words, to extract tiny, gelatinous drops of meaning. All very important and useful no doubt, but useful to *you* as well, as long as it distracts them from seeing the broad and beautiful picture of God walking the earth as a real man.

So *real*, Lucifer! Such a lover of natural things, such a mixture of all the emotions, such a despiser of sin, such a tender and compassionate lover of the small people and sinners who had nothing to offer him but their own need. Such a brave sufferer at the end when friendship and the richness of life said 'Stay', but destiny and obedience said that the cross could not be avoided. He was and is a good chap, Lucifer, and I love him. Oh, I know I'll go on making mistakes! And I know you won't give up. I know that every time I find a genuine pearl of truth you're going to send a bin-load of rubbish tumbling down to bury and obscure it. That's a real winner with people like me who so easily step backwards into cynicism. But I *am* learning – learning to ignore me and listen to him. A small, quiet sureness has taken root in me, and I'm relying on him to make sure that it grows.

The thing is, Lucifer, that I've been down in the dark for a long time. I've tasted hell, and I know what it is. It's the fear, the knowledge in your case, that God will never be able to smile at you again, that you've lost the only thing really worth having – the love of God. And I know now why you are so bitterly, cruelly determined to prevent as many as possible from finding peace. It's because you've lost it, isn't it? You wanted more than it's possible to have, and you lost everything. Jesus will never smile at you again, and all that's left is the endless striving to suck others into the loveless vacuum that you inhabit.

But out in the rain, just now, I was thinking. In the night (are there darker, deeper nights in endless night?) do you ever discover in yourself enough microscopic traces of shame and longing to make up a single tear of genuine remorse, no bigger, perhaps, than one of those fertile drops of rain falling so copiously on and around me? If so, then I think that even you could be saved, Lucifer. I fear, though, that the last spot of moisture dried and disappeared in you a very long time ago.

I remain, through God's grace, Never Yours,

Adrian Plass

Silver Birches

A Novel

Adrian Plass, Internationally Bestselling Author

When David Herrick receives an invitation to a reunion from a long-forgotten acquaintance, his first reaction is to refuse. He isn't feeling very sociable since his wife, Jessica, died six months ago.

But the invitation comes from Angela, one of his wife's oldest friends – and mysteriously, she has something for him from his beloved Jessica. Reluctant but curious, he visits Headly Manor.

When the friends gather, they no longer resemble the fresh-faced group of twenty years ago. One has been deserted by her husband, another has lost his faith, and another is filled with anger and bitterness. As they have less than forty-eight hours with each other, they decide to be vulnerable and bear their souls.

This poignant and moving story blends Adrian Plass's rich style of writing with his knack for addressing the deep issues we all face, such as faith, grief, love … and fear.

Softcover: 978-0-310-29203-6

Pick up a copy at your favorite bookstore or online!

ZONDERVAN®
.com

The Sacred Diary of Adrian Plass, Aged 37¾

Adrian Plass

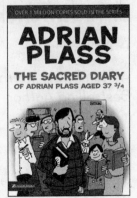

Saturday, December 14th

Feel led to keep a diary. A sort of spiritual log for the benefit of others in the future. Each new divine insight and experience will shine like a beacon in the darkness!

Can't think of anything to put in today.

Still, tomorrow's Sunday. Must be something on a Sunday, surely?

―――――――

Adrian Plass is hilarious, pure and simple. His readers are legion – and this is the bestselling book that started it all, converting thousands of people who love to laugh into avid Plass readers.

The Sacred Diary of Adrian Plass, Aged 37¾, is merriment and facetiousness at its best – a journal of the wacky Christian life of Plass's fictional alter ego, who chronicles in his 'sacred' diary the daily goings-on in the lives of ordinary-but-somewhat-eccentric people he knows and meets. Reading it will doeth good like a medicine!

Softcover: 978-0-310-26912-0

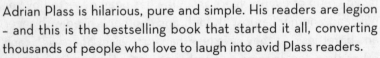

Pick up a copy at your favorite bookstore or online!

ZONDERVAN®
.com